Pronunciation
in the Classroom

THE **OVERLOOKED** ESSENTIAL

EDITED BY Tamara Jones

FOREWORD BY **JUDY B. GILBERT**

 tesol press

CONTENTS

FOREWORD

Judy B. Gilbert

Why Is Pronunciation Important?

When I was at university, I asked my Spanish teacher, a native speaker of the language, how I could improve my spoken Spanish. She answered, "If all you're interested in is the spoken language, go to a country where they speak it." Practical advice, but I never forgot the beginning of that remark. It seemed to assume that the spoken language was somehow less prestigious or important than the written. The fact is that most of our students *do* want to be able to use the language they are studying to speak with other people. Poor intelligibility and its likely companion, poor listening comprehension, can be socially inhibiting and damaging to a learner's ability to cope effectively in an English-speaking environment.

A Brief History of Pronunciation Teaching

Speech goes back to human beginnings; writing is relatively recent. So language teaching must have been mostly oral for thousands of years. But when Guttenberg invented movable type, this shifted language teaching to print for hundreds of years.

Then, in the late 19th century, serious scholars such as Henry Sweet began to study the spoken language itself. This brought speech back to a central place in language teaching. Robins (1967), in a history of linguistics, wrote:

> Descriptive phonetics . . . received powerful reinforcement from the . . . emphasis on living languages and on the inadequacy of the letters of dead languages in giving information on their actual pronunciation. Never again could there be an excuse for confusing written letters with spoken sound. (p. 186)

A major development occurred in 1918. Daniel Jones, who was the model for George Bernard Shaw's character Henry Higgins (Collins & Mees, 1999), published

An Outline of English Phonetics. This was the first such description of the standard pronunciation of any language.

> It is safe to say that no single individual has ever had such a profound influence upon methods of language learning as Daniel Jones. Unlike many of his contemporaries in early days, he believed that it was not enough to be able to read a foreign language and that it was of tremendous importance how one spoke it. It was this conviction that led him to develop methods of teaching . . . which eventually revolutionized the learning of languages and particularly the study of pronunciation and intonation. (Fry, 1968, p. 198)

However, in the 1960s there was a major shift in language teaching theory to a communicative approach. In the process—perhaps as a reaction to overreliance on meaning-free minimal pair drilling—pronunciation as a whole was dumped overboard. This caused phonetic research and the teaching of the spoken language to become disconnected, resulting in decades in which pronunciation has been an orphan in teacher training (Deng et al., 2009; Derwing & Munro, 2005; Gilbert, 2010; Macdonald, 2002; Murphy, 1997; Rossiter, Derwing, Manantim, & Thomson, 2010). Kelly (1969) referred to spoken language as the Cinderella of foreign language teaching.

The picture began to change in the 1990s. Samuda (1993) described the confusion in curriculum of the time, as programs tried to fit pronunciation in somewhere: either as a separate component, a series of self-paced, individualized modules, or integrated throughout the curriculum. As these alternatives were debated, she wrote that

> many of us quietly go about our work erroneously assuming that someone else is taking care of pronunciation. One reason we have been willing to overlook pronunciation instruction may stem, not so much from uncertainty about where it belongs in the curriculum, but from a basic uncertainty about how to teach it. (p. 757)

The Times They Are a-Changin' (Dylan, 1964)

In the 21st century, research and teacher training have begun to come together again, with a new recognition of the importance of the spoken language. Because there is always a shortage of time (and energy) and because teaching too much is generally counterproductive, the essential question is priorities: What elements of speech really need to be taught first? Any extra time can be used for other aspects of speech, but the central importance of prosody (rhythm and melody) must come first.

Why Is Prosody Central?

> Listeners use prosodic cues to confirm if an item is new or one that they are already aware of, to track important information, and to predict when one topic is ending and another is beginning. (Kang & Pickering, 2011, p. 6)

All languages must have a way to signal these elements, but English depends on the prosody. Here are two examples of the way other languages signal an "important word":

English/Japanese (post-word particle –*ga*)
THIS is my bag.
Kore-ga watashino kaban-desu.

English/Spanish (grammatical construction: mainly word order)
No, it's HIS fault.
Al contrario, la culpa la tiene él.

Because English depends mainly on the prosodic signals, speaking without these cues is baffling for the listener. Also, inability to notice these cues leads to poor listening comprehension. Speaking and listening are two sides of the same coin.

> Whereas, phonemic interference involves the identification of meaning-bearing linguistic units, a necessary step in the decoding of the message, prosodic interference inhibits the transmission of meaning itself, often negating or contradicting the intentions of the speaker. (Nash, 1971, p. 138)

Allen (1971) urged that intonation should be given primary attention. She wrote that instruction would be more effective if it

> (1) directs attention to a very few major patterns, (2) alerts the student to specific differences between the punctuation system and the intonation system, (3) distinguishes between the intonation of isolated sentences and the intonation of extended discourse, and (4) *teaches the student to think in terms of the speaker's intention in any given speech situation.* (p. 73, emphasis added)

Virginia Allen was a founding member of TESOL, and the above paragraph was the beginning of my own approach to teaching pronunciation.

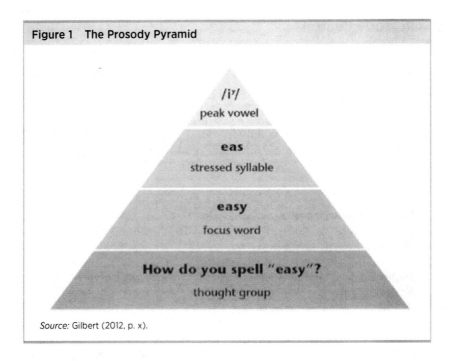

Figure 1   The Prosody Pyramid

/iʸ/
peak vowel

eas
stressed syllable

easy
focus word

How do you spell "easy"?
thought group

Source: Gilbert (2012, p. x).

After many years of trying to make English intonation/suprasegmentals/prosody easier to teach, I began to use the image in Figure 1. The foundation of the pyramid is the thought group (a short sentence, clause, or phrase). Each thought group has one focus word, and each focus word has one primary stressed syllable. The vowel at the energy peak of this syllable is the peak of information.

Where Should Pronunciation Fit?

In the following Introduction, Tamara Jones explains specifically what students need to know about pronunciation. Programs rarely have the luxury of stand-alone pronunciation classes, but once a teacher understands what elements are highest priority, they will be readily apparent in regular class content. These elements help bring clarity to text, and the following examples are easy to spot once you are looking for them: vowel clarity and lengthening (in crucial syllables), consonants that signal grammar cues (spelled with final letter D or S), word stress (helping identify the word), contrastive sentence emphasis (showing coherence—what goes with what), thought grouping (helping clarify grammatical divisions), and linking (helping tie thought groups together). Ways of promoting attention to crucial pronunciation of these elements in the regular classroom is the purpose of this book.

And finally, a statement about the importance of prosody: "It don't mean a thing if it ain't got that swing" (Ellington, 1931).

References

Allen, V. (1971). Teaching intonation, from theory to practice. *TESOL Quarterly, 5*, 73–81.

Collins, B., & Mees I. (1999). *The real Professor Higgins: The life and career of Daniel Jones.* Berlin, Germany: Mouton de Gruyter.

Deng, J., Holtby, A., Howden-Weaver, L., Nessim, L., Nicholas, B., Nickle, K., . . . Sun, M. (2009). *English pronunciation research: The neglected orphan of second language acquisition studies?* (Working Paper WPO5-9). Alberta, Canada: University of Alberta.

Derwing, T., & Munro, M. (2005). Second language accent and pronunciation teaching: A research-based approach. *TESOL Quarterly, 39*, 379–397.

Dylan, B. (1963). Times they are a-changin. On *Times they are a-changin* [Record]. Burbank, CA: Warner Bros. (1964)

Fry, D. (1968). Daniel Jones (obituary). *English Language Teaching, 22*, 198–199.

Gilbert, J. (2010). Pronunciation as orphan: What can be done? *Speak Out!, 43*, 3–7.

Gilbert, J. (2012). *Clear speech* (4th ed.). New York, NY: Cambridge University Press.

Kang, O., & Pickering, L. (2011). The role of objective measures of suprasegmental features in judgments of comprehensibility and oral proficiency in L2 spoken discourse. *Speak Out!, 44*, 4–8.

Kelly, G. (1969). *25 centuries of language teaching.* Rowley, MA: Newbury House.

Macdonald, S. (2002). Pronunciation—Views and practices of reluctant teachers. *Prospect, 17*(3), 3–18.

Mills, I. (1931). It don't mean a thing (if it ain't got that swing) [Recorded by D. Ellington]. On *It don't mean a thing (If it ain't got that swing)*. Chicago, IL: Brunswick Records. (1932)

Murphy, J. (1997). Phonology courses offered by MATESOL programs in the U.S. *TESOL Quarterly, 31*, 741–764.

Nash, R. (1971). Phonemic and prosodic interference and their effects on intelligibility. *International Congress of Phonetic Sciences, 7*, 138–139.

Robins, R. (1967). *A short history of linguistics.* London, England: Longman.

Rossiter, M., Derwing, T., Manantim, G., & Thomson, R. (2010). Oral fluency: The neglected component in the communicative language. *Canadian Modern Language Review, 66*, 583–606.

Samuda, V. (1993). Book notices. *TESOL Quarterly, 27*, 757–776.

The Gap Between the Integration of Pronunciation and Real Teaching Contexts

Where Are We Now?

For many years, I taught English in a variety of contexts without having a clear idea of how to teach pronunciation. I found the IPA intimidating and, never having been trained to teach pronunciation, I avoided bringing it up in class except to offer awkward correction when students mispronounced the /r/ sound. It wasn't until I was asked to take over an intermediate pronunciation class when a popular teacher left the program where I was an adjunct that I realized that, in fact, teaching pronunciation wasn't as scary as I had thought. On the contrary, it was fun, and the students really appreciated whatever help they could get. In fact, I started to realize that it wasn't just the students in my pronunciation class who would benefit from this instruction; students in many of my other classes needed it, too.

Sadly, I suspect that many other ESL and EFL teachers might have the same concerns about teaching pronunciation as I had in the beginning. Research conducted by Murphy (1997, 2014), Breitkreutz, Derwing, and Rossiter (2001), and Baker (2011) suggests that, by and large, teachers feel ill prepared to teach pronunciation. "One recurring theme [in the research] was that many teachers are hesitant when it comes to teaching pronunciation due to inexperience, lack of specialized training, lack of resources and/or lack of institutional support" (Murphy, 2014, p. 205). In my case, it was almost a perfect storm of all of these factors that had caused me to feel anxious about teaching pronunciation and avoid all but the very minimal instruction in my lessons.

In addition to the reality that pronunciation is underrepresented in teacher education, systematic pronunciation instruction takes a further hit because few ESL and EFL programs offer pronunciation-specific classes. As a result, educators are forced to integrate it into already overfilled curricula in other skill areas. Foote, Holtby, and Derwing (2011) found that the majority of teachers in adult ESL programs they surveyed devote only 6% of their class time to teaching pronunciation and correcting pronunciation-related errors, and Foote, Trofimovich, Collins, and Urzúa (2013) determined that much of this time is spent focusing on segmentals.

These results are dismaying when one considers the importance of pronunciation in communication. While a listener may be able to navigate a sentence littered with grammar errors, a breakdown in pronunciation can stop a conversation in its tracks. So why do we as teachers spend so much more time on things like grammar in our lessons? According to Kanellou (2009), one of the main reasons may be the fact that the texts we use often give scant consideration to pronunciation. Grant (2014a) points out that,

> when pronunciation is routinely relegated to token "listen and repeat" exercises at the end of chapters, students and teachers are apt to develop a simplistic view of pronunciation teaching and learning or to perceive pronunciation as incidental to oral proficiency. (p. ix)

It is no wonder I had avoided teaching pronunciation for so many years. If it is true that "the English sound system cannot be learned (and thus should not be taught) in a vacuum" (Celce-Murcia, Brinton, & Goodwin, 2010, p. 365), the real issue that teachers currently contend with is that of integration, of figuring out how to incorporate pronunciation seamlessly into their lesson plans. It is precisely with this issue in mind that this handbook for teachers was created.

What Do Teachers Need to Know?

When I cracked open the course book for my very first pronunciation class, I felt as though I had to learn a whole new language in order to teach the material. While this was slightly intimidating, I also found it thrilling, like I was learning the passwords that let me into a secret world. In order to fully access the suggestions in the following chapters, it is necessary for readers to understand that English pronunciation is often divided into two categories: segmentals and suprasegmentals.

Segmentals

Several years ago, I was lying on the table in my osteopath's office in Brussels listening to him talking about a professional workshop he had attended. As he described the course, he kept mentioning a breeding program he had participated in. It was not until a few minutes later that I realized that, in fact, he meant a *breathing* program, but he had substituted /d/ for /ð/. This is an example of sound functioning in *contrastive distribution*, "as minimally distinctive units of sound that can alter the meaning of a word" (Celce-Murcia et al., 2010, p. 51). The term *segmentals* describes phonemes (sounds), many of which can cause misunderstandings when mispronounced and which so intimidated me when I first started teaching. Segmentals are divided into consonant and vowel sounds.

CONSONANT SOUNDS. In order to raise money for my local scuba club, I once volunteered to sell hot dogs and hamburgers with some of the other club members. One of the volunteers was from France, and he started the day asking people if they wanted an 'otdog or an 'amburger. He became aware of his mistake and worked through the afternoon, not only selling food, but also pronouncing the initial /h/ sound on both words. Consonant sounds are distinguished by whether they are voiced or not (think of the contrast between /f/ and/v/), where they are formed in the mouth (think about how you stick your tongue between your teeth to make the /ð/ and /θ/ sounds), and how the airflow is affected (think about how the air is stopped when you say /p/ but not /m/). Learners not only substitute sounds erroneously, as my osteopath did, and omit sounds, as the scuba club member did, but they may also add sounds, as in "eschool" (/ɜsku:l/) instead of "school" if the speaker has difficulty navigating *consonant clusters*, when two or more consonants appear together, like /sk/. These errors may depend on the L1 of the learner; however, "contrary to popular belief, not all segmental difficulties are language-specific" (Grant, 2014b, p. 20).

VOWEL SOUNDS. Just the other day, one of my students asked me for a pink pepper. As she stood in front of my desk with scissors in her hand, I immediately understood that, in fact, she wanted some pink paper. She had inadvertently substituted the vowel /eɪ/ with /ɛ/. Vowel sounds "are produced by a freely flowing airstream. Essentially, we create different vowel sounds by using the mouth as a resonance cavity and changing its size and shape" (Grant, 2014b, p. 21). Experts categorize vowel sounds as *simple vowels* (those without a glide movement, such as the /ɛ/ in "pepper"), *glide vowels* (those that have an accompanying /y/ or /w/, like the /eɪ/ in "paper"), and *diphthongs* (two vowel sounds in the same syllable, such as /ɔɪ/ as in "boy"). There are also distinctions commonly made between *rounded* versus *spread* vowels (in terms of lip position) and *tense* versus *lax* vowels (in terms of muscle tension).

SCHWA. Recently, when I was helping students learn vocabulary for their math lessons, I heard a student say she wanted to make sure the line. I waited for her to finish her sentence. Make sure the line . . . what? Was straight? Was long enough? Actually, she had wanted to "measure" the line. In other words, she had attempted to clearly pronounce both of the vowel sounds in "measure," which resulted in a misunderstanding. While vowel sounds are notoriously difficult for students to master, the most significant challenge for students lies in the fact that the pronunciation of a vowel changes depending on where it is in a word or sentence. In other words, when a vowel appears in an unstressed syllable, like the second syllable of "mea-sure," it is generally reduced to the schwa sound, or /ə/. "Vowel reduction is particularly baffling for students whose L1 [first language] never reduces vowels, such as Spanish and Japanese. Learning to hear the difference between clear and reduced vowels is therefore a challenging but essential task" (Gilbert, 2008, p. 17).

Suprasegmentals

Also known as *prosody*, the term *suprasegmentals* refers to the "features of pronunciation that stretch over more than one sound or segment" (Grant, 2014b, p. 16). In other words, suprasegmentals encompass everything beyond individual sounds. Miller (2011) refers to suprasegmentals as *core pronunciation features* because they are so vital to communication. Many experts feel that "while segmental instruction may still be important for accent reduction in the long run, it is essential to give priority to prosody in pronunciation since it results in better comprehensibility in the short run" (Celce-Murcia et al., 2010, p. 33). In many pronunciation textbooks on the market, suprasegmentals are divided into word stress, rhythm, prominence, thought groups, linking, and final intonation.

WORD STRESS. I was recently on a hike in Malaysia, and our guide was trying to explain the reason he was unable to give us the passes for the mountain. He apologized and said that the "mission" wasn't working. After a few moments, I understood that, in fact, the "machine" used for printing was broken. The breakdown occurred simply because the guide said "MAchine" instead of "maCHINE." A syllable has a vowel sound at its core and possibly consonant sounds on either side of it. The word "machine" has two syllables, /mə/ and /ʃin/. Problems can arise for students who add additional syllables to a word ("church" becomes "church-ee") or cut syllables from a word ("tofu" become "tof") because of interference from the speaker's L1. In polysyllabic words, the vowel sounds of the *stressed syllables*, which Gilbert (2008) refers to as *peak vowels*, are often pronounced more clearly, that is, longer, louder, and higher in pitch. When a speaker stresses the wrong syllable, breakdowns can occur because proficient English speakers mentally "store words under stress patterns . . . and we find it difficult to interpret an utterance in which a word is pronounced with the wrong stress pattern—we begin to 'look up' possible words under this wrong stress pattern" (Brown, 1990, p. 51).

RHYTHM. Many years ago, when I was an undergrad, I had a professor whose lectures had a sedative effect on me. It wasn't that the subject matter was particularly dull; my tendency to nod off resulted because when he spoke, he read every single word in a monotone. In order to "maintain the interest of the listener" (Cauldwell,

2007), the professor shouldn't have read directly from his notes, as his delivery eliminated all traces of rhythm from his speech. Many pronunciation texts refer to rhythm as *sentence stress* to describe the tendency in English to stress content words and reduce function words. In other words, content words, including nouns, main verbs, adjectives, adverbs, question words, demonstrative and possessive pronouns, long conjunctions, negative words, and the prepositions in phrasal verbs, "usually receive stress because of their semantic as well as syntactic salience" (Celce-Murcia et al., 2010, p. 210). However, function words, such as articles, auxiliary verbs and the copula *to be*, short conjunctions, prepositions, and pronouns, are usually unstressed. Due to an emphasis on written grammar in many ESL and EFL programs,

> it is common for students to emphasize every word when they are anxious to be understood. This gives the appearance of agitation or insistence that they may not intend, and it certainly diminishes the effectiveness of the prosodic "road signs" that the listener needs. (Gilbert, 2008, p. 14)

PROMINENCE. "The name is Bond. James Bond." This might very well be one of the most famous lines to ever come out of Hollywood, but it is also a great example of the use of prominence, or focus. While many languages use grammar or syntax to highlight important information, English does this largely through pitch contours. In other words, when those of us who are proficient English speakers want listeners to pay attention to key information in a thought group, we change the pitch of the stressed syllable of the word, lengthen the vowel sound of the stressed syllable, and make that vowel sound clearer while reducing the other vowel sounds, often to /ə/. We do this to contrast between old information and new information, as in "**BOND. JAMES** Bond." In the first sentence, "Bond" is the new information and so receives the stress. In the second sentence, "James" is the new information and "Bond" is old information, so "James" is said with more stress. We also use prominence to both agree enthusiastically ("you **DO** LIKE ICE CREAM!") and correct or contrast ("my **FIRST** NAME is TAMara"). Students who struggle to hear focus, as well as those who hear it but don't ascribe any significance to it, may be missing out on valuable information that is communicated through these pitch contours.

THOUGHT GROUPS. When I was working on my doctoral research, I had to read many texts about the philosophy of language. I noticed that whenever I would encounter a long, complicated sentence, I often read the sentence aloud to make sense of it. By breaking the sentences, which could take up as much as half a page, into manageable chunks, it was easier to make sense of the authors' arguments. Simply put, thought groups, also known as *speech groups*, are groups of words that go together syntactically and grammatically and are bound on either side by brief pauses. Miller (2011) refers to this chunking as *auditory punctuation*. If speakers do not break down their longer utterances, their message may be very difficult to understand, just as a paragraph without punctuation would be difficult to decipher.

LINKING. Several years ago, a student complained of being in a fast food restaurant and ordering a meal, only to be faced with the bewildering response "Latbefrererdogo?" Of course, he had absolutely no idea that the server had been asking him if he wanted his meal to eat there or to go. Proficient English speakers, like the McDonald's worker in my student's story, tend to run words together, often creating new sounds and deleting others. As Celce-Murcia et al. (2010) point out,

> the ability to speak English "smoothly," to utter words or syllables that are appropriately connected, entails the use of linking (or liaison), which is the connection of the final sound of one word to the initial sound of the next. (p. 165)

Speakers often link words when the consonant sounds are the same or similar, as in "some money"; when the last sound of a word is a consonant sound and the first sound of the following word is a vowel sound, as in "get into"; and when the last sound of a word is a vowel and the first sound of the following word is a vowel, as in "go(w)away" and "high(y)and." Unfamiliarity with linking is one of the biggest barriers to listening comprehension (Field, 2003), and if students don't apply linking to their own speech, it can sound choppy and lack fluency.

FINAL INTONATION. I used to have a great dry cleaner from Korea. Whenever I would leave his shop, he would say, "Thank you very much. Please come again." While his words communicated a friendly message, he applied a Korean intonation pattern to them, so he actually sounded quite the opposite. This was because the pitch of his voice fell more deeply and fell in a different place than a proficient English speaker's would have when uttering the same sentences. In fact, intonation "has the power to reinforce, mitigate, or even undermine the words spoken" (Wichmann, 2005, p. 229). Simply put, intonation is the rise and fall in the pitch of the voice within a thought group. Usually, when making a statement or expressing certainty, a speaker will fall after the focus word. When asking a yes/no question or expressing uncertainty, a speaker will rise after the focus word. Finally, when a speaker has more to say, he or she will communicate this by using a flat pitch, except when listing. However, many experts, including Rogerson-Revell (2012), contend that intonation can be an extremely difficult skill to both teach and master. Perhaps this is because the rules associated with pitch levels are baffling to many educators and the relationship between pitch and attitude can be difficult to explain and because, as researchers such as Stibbard (2001) argue, the connection between attitude and intonation is context-specific.

How Can We Integrate Pronunciation Into All Our Lessons?

It is rare that teachers have the opportunity, as I did, to teach a stand-alone pronunciation class (Foote, Holtby, & Derwing, 2011) and really learn about English prosody instruction. More commonly,

> teachers must balance the needs of their students within a somewhat fixed curriculum. If this is the case, pronunciation is not always explicitly included even in a speaking course, and teachers need to find ways to integrate pronunciation into existing curriculum and textbook materials. (Celce-Murcia, Brinton, & Goodwin, 2010, p. 381)

Nonetheless, instructors do, by and large, agree that pronunciation is an important component of an ESL, EFL, or English as a lingua franca curriculum, and we tend to generally believe that the pronunciation instruction we incorporate into our lessons can be effective (Foote et al., 2011). The question this book aims to answer is: What are the best ways to do this?

To begin, as Ahmad and Burri, Baker, and Acton point out in Chapters 1 and 2, words are the building blocks of language. After all, "while without grammar very little can be conveyed, without vocabulary nothing can be conveyed" (Wilkins, 1972, p. 111). Learning about word stress serves two important purposes for students: It helps them hear the words when they are used in a conversation, and it helps them use the words comprehensibly themselves. Moreover, pronunciation instruction creates the potential for multiple passes over new vocabulary, something that is essential for a language learner to take genuine ownership of new words (Nation, 2001). For these reasons, we are doing our students no favors if we introduce new vocabulary without simultaneously integrating pronunciation instruction.

Pronunciation is also an integral part of oral communication, so it is a natural fit for speaking and listening classes. In Chapters 3, 4, 5, and 6, the authors stress the importance of including prosodic features, specifically prominence, intonation, and thought groups, into classes that emphasize listening and speaking skill development. In Chapter 3, Muller Levis and Levis describe a series of interactive activities that provide students with practice applying the intonation patterns (both final and prominent) expected by North American English speakers. In Chapter 4, Sardegna, Chiang, and Ghosh discuss the connection between pronunciation, specifically prominence, and presentation skills. They suggest several activities that help students move toward greater comprehensibility and autonomy in their public speaking. Thoughts groups and prominence also feature significantly in Murphy's discussion in Chapter 5 about integrating pronunciation into listening lessons. Key to comprehension and memory (Harley, 2000) as well as turn taking, thought groups are an essential aspect of listening instruction. In addition, exposing students to strategies for dealing with compressed speech is a priority for teachers of listening, as learners are often hindered by "arguably the commonest perceptual cause of breakdown of understanding: namely, lexical segmentation, the identification of words in connected speech" (Field, 2003, p. 327). In Chapter 6, Reed focuses on the important role that prominence plays in the illocutionary force of an utterance. Unfortunately, learners may neither hear the pitch contour nor be aware that it carries meaning; thus, they may be missing out on important information other listeners have heard. Clearly, intelligible pronunciation is crucial to both speaking and listening. However, oral communications teachers "often address pronunciation unsystematically, applying it primarily as a corrective measure when errors are too prominent to be ignored" (Levis & Grant, 2003, p. 13). These chapters suggest a more systematic approach for incorporating pronunciation into the listening and speaking curriculum.

The authors of Chapters 7, 8, and 9 contend that pronunciation merges remarkable easily into grammar lessons. Perhaps this is because when the target grammar is incorporated into pronunciation exercises, it is "mutually reinforcing: practicing pronunciation with similar grammar and vocabulary activities as those found in the course should help to fix lexical and syntactic aspects" (Chela-Flores, 2001, p. 87). In Chapter 7, Miller and Jones advocate for the inclusion of pronunciation into beginning-level grammar classes. Beginners benefit from exposure to pronunciation norms in the form of a prosody package, as "it makes little sense to immerse beginning learners into the grammar and vocabulary of English but then leave them to struggle on their own with the pronunciation" (Zielinski & Yates, 2014, p. 59). In Chapter 8, Floyd suggests a variety of activities that teachers can use when integrating intermediate grammar and pronunciation, both segmental and suprasegmental. In Chapter 9, Rimmer points out that since many ESL and EFL syllabi are organized around grammar skills (Foote et al., 2011), it makes sense for the existing curricula to absorb pronunciation practice rather than vice versa. Although the same pronunciation skills may be recycled level after level, the "development of speaking skills is not a hierarchically determined process" (Keys, 2000, p. 97). Therefore, the recycling of pronunciation skills with progressively more difficult target structures reinforces both the grammar and the pronunciation.

Finally, Chapters 10, 11, and 12 make a strong case for the integration of pronunciation into lessons that focus on reading and spelling. Although at first light reading may not seem to be an obvious match for pronunciation, in Chapter 10 Woo and Price demonstrate the benefits of incorporating phonics instruction into reading lessons from the very start. They argue that in order for students to become skilled readers, they need "knowledge of phonemic segmentation, letter-sound correspondences, and spelling patterns to bond the complete spellings of specific words to their pronunciations and meanings in memory" (Ehri, 2003, p. 2). In Chapter 11 Han also argues in favor of including pronunciation instruction in the reading curriculum, though at the passage level. She presents activities that help students develop strategies for three major types of passage-level reading: extensive reading, speed reading, and repeated reading. Finally, in Chapter 11, Brown describes how pronunciation can enhance instruction in spelling and punctuation.

> It is important for ESL and EFL teachers to understand the correspondences between English phonology and English orthography so that they can teach their learners (1) how to predict the pronunciation of a word given its spelling and (2) how to come up with a plausible spelling for a word given its pronunciation. (Celce-Murcia et al., 2010, p. 419)

The activities suggested by Brown can help students master both of these goals, as well as highlight a valuable connection between prosody and punctuation.

Who Is a Pronunciation Teacher?

Although pronunciation skills are separated into tidy categories for the sake of clarity, they are, in reality, a much messier pile of overlapping concepts. Just as it would be difficult to teach writing without having students learn about grammar and spelling, it is impossible for students to apply prominence, for example, if they haven't been exposed to thought groups, speech rhythm, word stress, and peak vowels. Therefore, it makes much more sense for teachers to integrate pronunciation into lessons on a consistent basis. Just like we teach elements of grammar and then spend months, if not years, revising them, so should we touch on these core pronunciation features again and again. Furthermore, pronunciation should not be confined to classes specifically designated as such. Students need to be able to communicate in all of their subjects, and "intelligible pronunciation is an essential component of communicative competence" (Morley, 1991, p. 488).

However, I know many of you may be hesitant to introduce pronunciation into your lessons, as I once was. If you are a nonnative English speaker, you may feel even more apprehensive due to insecurity about your own pronunciation. Interestingly, however, many experts argue that nonnative-English-speaking teachers make excellent teachers of pronunciation because they can provide an attainable model for students and their personal experiences with learning English can inform their teaching. In addition, whether you are a native or nonnative English speaker, perhaps you worry, as I did, that you are not prepared to teach pronunciation as "most training and degree programs have been doing a less-than-adequate job of preparing ESL and EFL teachers in this area" (Murphy, 2014, p. 204). I hope that by reading this book you get some useful and practical ideas that you can implement straight away, no matter what classes you teach.

Therefore, I would argue that regardless of specific courses taught, first language, or educational background, *all* ESL and EFL teachers are pronunciation teachers.

References

Baker, A. A. (2011). Discourse prosody and teachers' stated beliefs and practices. *TESOL Journal, 2/3,* 263–292.

Breitkreutz, J., Derwing, T. M., & Rossiter, M. J. (2001). Pronunciation teaching practices in Canada. *TESL Canada Journal, 19,* 51–61.

Brown, G. (1990). *Listening to spoken English*. London, England: Longman.

Cauldwell, R. (2007, March). *Computer technology in teaching speaking and pronunciation*. Paper presented at the annual convention of TESOL, Seattle, WA.

Celce-Murcia, M., Brinton, D., & Goodwin, J. (2010). *Teaching pronunciation: A course book and reference guide*. New York, NY: Cambridge University Press.

Chela-Flores, B. (2001). Pronunciation and language learning: And integrative approach. *International Review of Applied Linguistics in Language Teaching, 39*(2), 85–101.

Ehri, L. C. (2003, March). *Systematic phonics instruction: Findings of the National Reading Panel*. Paper presented at the invitational seminar organized by the Standards and Effectiveness Unit, Department for Education and Skills, British Government, London, England.

Field, J. (2003). Promoting perception: Lexical segmentation in L2 listening. *ELT Journal, 57,* 325–334.

Foote, J. A., Holtby, A. K., & Derwing, T. M. (2011). Survey of the teaching of pronunciation in adult ESL programs in Canada, 2010. *TESL Canada Journal, 29*(1), 1–22.

Foote, J. A., Trofimovich, P., Collins, L., & Urzúa, F. (2013). Pronunciation teaching practices in communicative second language classes. *Language Learning Journal*. Advance online publication. doi:10.1080/09571736.2013.784345

Gilbert, J. (2008). *Teaching pronunciation: Using the prosody pyramid*. Cambridge, England: Cambridge University Press.

Grant, L. (2014a). Introduction. In L. Grant (Ed.), *Pronunciation myths*. Ann Arbor: University of Michigan Press, vii–xi.

Grant, L. (2014b). Prologue to the myths: What teachers need to know. In L. Grant (Ed.), *Pronunciation myths*. Ann Arbor: University of Michigan Press, 1–33.

Harley, B. (2000). Listening strategies in ESL: Do age and LI make a difference? *TESOL Quarterly, 34,* 769–777.

Keys, K. J. (2000). Discourse level phonology in the language curriculum: A review of current thinking in teaching pronunciation in EFL courses. *Linguagem and Ensino, 3*(1), 89–105.

Kanellou, V. (2009). The practice of pronunciation teaching in current ELT manuals and handbooks: A review. *SPEAK OUT!, 40,* 18–21.

Levis, J., & Grant, L. (2003). Integrating pronunciation into ESL/EFL classrooms, *TESOL Journal, 12*(2), 13–21.

Miller, S. (2011, March). *Integrating pronunciation into beginning grammar classes.* Paper presented at the annual convention of TESOL, New Orleans, LA.

Morley, J. (1991). The pronunciation component in teaching English to speakers of other languages. *TESOL Quarterly, 25,* 481–520.

Murphy, J. (1997). Phonology Courses offered by MATESOL programs in the U.S. *TESOL Quarterly, 31,* 741–764.

Murphy, J. (2014). Myth 7: Teacher training programs provide adequate preparation in how to teach pronunciation. In L. Grant (Ed.), *Pronunciation myths.* Ann Arbor: University of Michigan Press, 188–224.

Nation, P. (2001). *Learning vocabulary in another language.* Cambridge, England: Cambridge University Press.

Rogerson-Revell, P. (2012). Can or should we teach intonation? *IATEFL Pronunciation SIG Newsletter, 47,* 16–20.

Stibbard, R. (2001). *Vocal expressions of emotions in non-laboratory speech* (Unpublished doctoral dissertation). University of Reading, England.

Wichmann, A. (2005). Please—From courtesy to appeal: The role of intonation in the expression of attitudinal meaning. *English Language and Linguistics, 9,* 229–253.

Wilkins, D. (1972). *Linguistics in language teaching.* London, England: Arnold.

Zielinksi, B., & Yates, L. (2014). Myth 2: Pronunciation instruction is not appropriate for beginning-level learners. In L. Grant (Ed.), *Pronunciation myths* (pp. 188–224). Ann Arbor: University of Michigan Press, 56–79.

CHAPTER 1

Integrating Pronunciation with Vocabulary Skills

Kay Ahmad

As an English as a second language instructor, I have experienced on several occasions in many different levels and types of classes that moment when a student is asking me a question or making a point, and there is one word that I just can't understand. We've all experienced this, so we know how important it is for our students to be understood not only in their classrooms but also at work and in the community. Providing pronunciation instruction in conjunction with vocabulary-focused learning activities is beneficial for our students' aural and oral interactions.

An important factor in learning vocabulary is focusing on intelligible pronunciation. Gilbert (2008) states that "English language learners tend to ignore stress when they learn vocabulary. And failure to learn the stress of new words often leads to an inability to recognize those words in spoken form" (p. 14). Without learning correct pronunciation of words and phrases, individuals can easily be misunderstood when speaking or can misunderstand the messages others are trying to convey to them. Pronunciation instruction gives students the opportunity to understand patterns associated with spoken English, such as patterns indicating word stress. By integrating pronunciation and vocabulary in the classroom, we help students develop a better awareness about these patterns and the ability to apply this knowledge as they are exposed to new words and expressions. When learning new words, there are several pronunciation features that should be incorporated in the learning process: word stress, vowel and consonant sounds, and word endings. When learning word combinations, including phrasal verbs, collocations, and idioms, understanding pronunciation features such as thought groups, rhythm, linking, and intonation is essential. This chapter further explains the importance of the incorporation of pronunciation instruction in vocabulary learning and provides examples of how to do this and resources that can be used in the teaching and learning of vocabulary and pronunciation.

Pronunciation and Words

Teaching and learning new vocabulary has traditionally focused primarily on the definitions and parts of speech, but pronunciation is clearly an important factor in learning new words. Thus, teachers should facilitate this learning by not only explaining definitions but also demonstrating the pronunciation of these words. In reference to the latter, wouldn't it be better to provide students with tools to facilitate intelligible pronunciation instead of just focusing on having students repeat after the teacher or dictionary recording? Word stress, vowel and consonant sounds, and word endings are pronunciation features that are relevant to teaching and learning new vocabulary.

Word Stress and Vowel Sounds

The Prosody Pyramid, developed by Gilbert (2008) to represent the English prosodic system, emphasizes the various interdependent levels of pronunciation: thought groups, focus word, stress, and peak syllable, which makes the rhythm of the English language. To facilitate the clear pronunciation of new vocabulary and avoid miscommunication in extended discourse, students need to have an understanding of how to pronounce the peak vowel sound clearly in the stressed syllable of a word, such as the /eɪ/ sound in *information*, and understand the other syllables in this word have reduced vowel sounds.

One technique to help students learn the vowel sounds is to associate each vowel sound with a specific word. All dictionaries include key words such as *hot* and *father* to demonstrate the /ɑ/ sound. However, those words are sometimes difficult to remember (especially for students at lower levels) and to reference when discussing the pronunciation of words. The Color Vowel™ Chart (Figure 1), a visual aid developed by Taylor and Thompson (1999/2015), connects the vowel sounds of English to key words and phrases and provides a shorthand for teachers and learners to talk about pronunciation with ease. This tool can be introduced to students even at the lowest levels and used throughout the class or program to focus learners' attention on the stressed vowel sounds in new words, thus helping them hear the stress that establishes the rhythmical patterns of spoken English. Students are introduced not only to the sounds but also to the positions of the sounds because the chart shape represents the mouth to show the sounds in relation to whether the sound is pronounced in the front, central part, or back of the mouth and whether the jaw is high or low.

Taylor and Thompson (n.d.) provide sample lessons to introduce the Color Vowel™ Chart at different levels. At lower levels, teachers can introduce a few sounds at a time. The purpose of this introductory lesson is to focus learners' attention on the stressed vowel sound of the words in the Color Vowel™ Chart and to develop the

Figure 1   The Color Vowel™ Chart

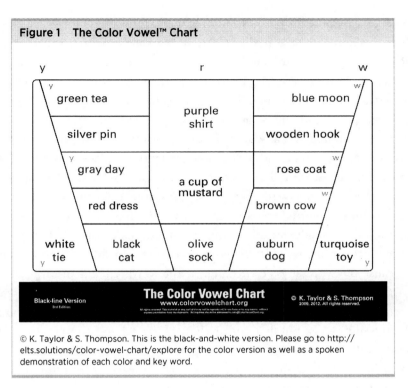

y   r   w

green tea	purple shirt	blue moon
silver pin		wooden hook
gray day	a cup of mustard	rose coat
red dress		brown cow
white tie	black cat	olive sock	auburn dog	turquoise toy

The Color Vowel Chart
www.colorvowelchart.org

Black-line Version
3rd Edition

© K. Taylor & S. Thompson
2009, 2012. All rights reserved.

All rights reserved. This material or any part of it may not be reproduced, in any form or by any means, without express permission from the claimants. All inquiries should be addressed to info@ColorVowelChart.org.

© K. Taylor & S. Thompson. This is the black-and-white version. Please go to http:// elts.solutions/color-vowel-chart/explore for the color version as well as a spoken demonstration of each color and key word.

connection between the sound and the color representing that sound. Learners can then transfer that knowledge to focusing on and discussing more easily the stressed vowel of new words and the peak vowel of phrases. To introduce the Color Vowel™ Chart at higher levels, a discovery activity can be done to help students determine where the vowels should be located on a blank chart. For example, students can clearly feel which vowels are pronounced with a more open mouth by placing their hands under their jaws while saying different vowel sounds. Moreover, they can use a lollipop or tongue depressor to determine whether the tongue moves to the front or the back of the mouth, which designates whether the sound is a front, central, or back vowel sound. Once students have completed the chart, the Color Vowel™ Chart can be introduced with a clearer understanding of why the chart is shaped as it is.

As students learn new words, referencing the Color Vowel™ Chart provides a common connection for the whole class when discussing vowel sounds. It's much easier to refer to the color GREEN when discussing the vowel pronunciation in *feel* or in the stressed syllable of *intervene* rather than just saying the sound /i/. Some common vowel mispronunciations include distinguishing between /i/ and /ɪ/. For instance, students often confuse the verbs *leave* (GREEN) and *live* (SILVER for the verb). Since these words are confused because they are similar in pronunciation, it would be beneficial to emphasize the difference in the vowel sounds and hopefully prevent future misusage because the pronunciation of these words was emphasized along with the differences in meaning. If students learn to associate /i/ with GREEN and /ɪ/ with SILVER, they should be able to better distinguish what they hear and what they are trying to say with more ease. There are various ways that students can demonstrate their understanding of vowel sounds using the colors. The teacher can review words with a vowel sound underlined, and students can say what color sound it is, write the color down, or match that word with the appropriate color word. For the latter, the words can be written on index cards and students can place the words under the index card of the color word that has that same sound. Taylor and Thompson (n.d.) have also suggested using wall charts or student notebooks to list which words or stressed syllables of words have the same vowel sounds as the colors. Additional ideas and resources can be found at http://elts.solutions/color-vowel-chart.

As students learn the word stress of more complex words, they can become confused because the word stress can change as the words change in form. For example, *psyCHOlogy* and *psychoLOgical* are stressed differently, which in turn changes the pronunciation of the vowel sounds. The first *o* in *psyCHOlogy* is stressed because it precedes the suffix –*logy*, but that same *o* changes to a schwa sound in *psych**o**LOgical*, and the second *o* is stressed because it precedes the suffix –*ical*. This is a shift in word stress, which is related to the suffix in each word. As teachers introduce new vocabulary, they should incorporate activities in which students investigate other word forms and shifts in word stress. A fun way for students to demonstrate the word stress is to say the word and stand up only for the stressed syllable. See Chapter 2 for more information and activities regarding word stress in word forms and Chapter 10 for suggestions for increasing the phonemic awareness of students as they learn to read.

The Schwa Sound

One important vowel sound is the schwa sound because every vowel and many vowel combinations can be reduced to the unstressed schwa sound /ə/, and this vowel reduction is a key to facilitating word stress and the rhythm of American English. It is important to note that this sound can also be a stressed vowel sound /ʌ/, especially in single-syllable words such as *but* and *love*, but the sound primarily functions as a reduced vowel sound in many prefixes, suffixes, multisyllabic words, and function words.

Students often have trouble recognizing the schwa sound and understanding what it sounds like. I have found a simple and humorous way to explain how this sound is made. I explain to my students that it is the sound a person typically makes when that person is hit in the stomach. As I physically demonstrate this, students are either shocked or amused, but they do remember. This is a sound that a teacher does not want to overemphasize in a word because that would interfere with the word stress, so the symbolic fist to the stomach can help students recall what sound needs to be used.

Consonants

In addition to vowel sounds, teachers can also focus on correct pronunciation of consonants and especially word endings of vocabulary being learned. Common pronunciation errors include the dropping of the final consonant sound of words or the mispronunciation of consonants and consonant clusters, especially for those consonants that have different pronunciations.

/g/ in **g**irl and /dʒ/ in **g**iraffe

/tʃ/ in **ch**ange, /k/ in stoma**ch**, and /ʃ/ in ma**ch**ine

/ft/ in lau**ght**er and /t/ in bou**ght**

Some consonant errors may not interfere too much with communication, but they could interrupt the communication as the listener thinks about what is actually trying to be conveyed in the conversation. As teachers discuss new words, exceptions to the typical pronunciation for consonants should be emphasized and demonstrated. Students could focus on a particular consonant and its various sounds either by brainstorming words with that consonant and categorizing those words by the sound of the consonant (higher level) or by sorting a set of vocabulary words with that consonant by sound (lower level). To incorporate meaning and pronunciation, students can create sentences, poems, or stories either individually or in groups to share orally with the rest of the class. A general activity that incorporates vocabulary and pronunciation involves giving oral homework such as having students read and record the sentences they created using new vocabulary words or words that they personally have difficulty pronouncing. Other examples of oral homework include tasks that relate to the theme of learning modules such as reading a poem or script, role-playing a situation, and stating an opinion (Mendez, 2010). Mendez (2010) also provides guidance and step-by-step instructions on how to implement oral assignments. Additionally, some oral assignments can be interactive, such as decision-making or problem-solving group discussions. One example is to determine from tourist information how and where to spend a day off or vacation as a group (Mendez, 2010).

Understanding the difference between voiced and voiceless sounds will help students better master the pronunciation of consonants and word endings. One common technique used by instructors to determine if a consonant is voiced is to have students touch their necks and feel for a vibration in their vocal chords. Another way is to have students clasp their hands over their ears and hear the vibration (Grant, 2010). For example, distinguishing the difference in pronunciation between *life*

(WHITE) and *live* (SILVER), which are often confused in usage, can be explained by stating that the two consonant sounds /f/ and /v/ are made in virtually the same way except that the /v/ includes a vibration when making the sound. Additionally, the vowel sounds in these two words are also different, as noted. Interestingly, some minimal pairs, contrasting in voiced and voiceless consonants, appear to have the same vowel sound, such as *leaf* and *leave*. However, the vowel sound is not exactly the same. Both vowel sounds are /i/ (GREEN), but the vowel sound before the voiced consonant /v/ is longer.

Websites can be used to help students distinguish and practice consonant and vowel sounds. The University of Iowa, in association with Grant's (2010) *Well Said* textbook, has a website and app that demonstrate how vowel and consonant sounds are produced (see http://soundsofspeech.uiowa.edu). Another website listed in the resources at the end of this chapter focuses on the pronunciation of diphthongs and triphthongs. Pronunciation software such as Pronunciation Power 1 and 2 (English Computerized Learning, n.d.) and Ellis Master Pronunciation (Pearson Education, 2015) are available for larger programs that provide computer-assisted language learning.

Exercises/Resources for Word Stress and Sounds in Words

Word stress and sounds are the basis of spoken vocabulary, and effective use of these pronunciation features ensures comprehensibility. Providing students with tools such as the Color Vowel™ Chart and explaining guidelines in understanding patterns in stress and sound production are beneficial instructional techniques for student learning. Brown (1994) states that "written English typically utilizes a greater variety of lexical items than spoken conversational English . . . because writing allows the writer more processing time" (p. 290). To transfer the vocabulary used in writing into learners' conversational English, learners need to develop the spoken aspects of the vocabulary as they are exposed to these words in reading and writing activities. One example is reading texts or their own written work out loud, which gives learners some practice in exploring the pronunciation features of new words and expressions as well as an opportunity for teachers to assist in correcting pronunciation errors. The following subsections present additional ways to integrate pronunciation (sounds and word stress) instruction with vocabulary skills.

WORD FAMILIES

At lower levels, students can benefit from associating vocabulary with pronunciation by using word families such as *CAT—bat, fat, hat, mat, pat, rat, sat.* Learning is enhanced when students can associate newly learned words with something that they have already learned. For example, if students learned about the /æ/ sound and the words *BLACK* **CAT** from the Color Vowel™ Chart, then they could focus on this sound by learning other words that have that sound. Connecting the sound to *cat* and then to other words ending in *–at* provide a word family that reinforces learners' understanding of this sound. Games incorporating one or more word families that help students focus on meaning and pronunciation can be created. For example, a simple board game could incorporate words and pictures in which a student would have to move to the corresponding picture for the word that she landed on. If the student lands on a picture, then she could move one space ahead if she says the word correctly.

Another example is a memory matching game in which students turn two cards over at a time and try to match the picture that represents the word. This matching game can incorporate a speaking component to help students practice speaking and listening to these minimal pairs such as *cat, bat, hat*, and so on. Thus, the student would not get the match unless he could say the word correctly. For words such as *pat* and *sat* that are difficult to exemplify in pictures, a variation of the matching could focus on matching words that belong to the same word family, such as matching *pat-sat* or *dish-fish*.

VOCABULARY SETS FOR LIFE SKILLS AND CONTENT-BASED LEARNING

Vocabulary sets are not learned in isolation. Instructors tend to incorporate vocabulary sets in association with particular life skills or content-based learning. For example, students learn numbers in adult ESL classes so that they can provide important personal numbers, write checks, follow recipes, and understand how much something costs. Understanding numbers is also needed in mathematics and history courses. These essential vocabulary words need to be understood and spoken intelligibly, so learning the pronunciation of numbers is just as important as learning and using the numbers (e.g., **sixteen** vs. **six**ty; see Chapter 8). Additional examples of pronunciation associated with particular vocabulary sets follows. Second language learners usually learn the vocabulary that is associated with the calendar. As students learn the days of the week, they can practice the pattern of stressing the first syllable in each word. However, when they learn the months of the year, they need to also focus on how many syllables the month has and which one is stressed, for example, distinguishing the stress rule for three-syllable months such as *November* from the varied stress patterns for two-syllable months such as **A**pril and Ju**ly**.

Learning new vocabulary is often associated with specific areas of study such as geography and history. Words can include proper names that are associated with a particular subject of study, such as learning the U.S. states or the names of U.S. presidents. As students learn these names, they can additionally focus on peak vowel sounds and word stress. Henry (1999) provides picture/pronunciation cards

Table 1	Example of Stress Patterns Chart for Student Exercise	
— °	— ° °	° — °
Nixon	**Wa**shington	No**vem**ber
Carter	**Ke**nnedy	De**cem**ber
April		
August		

of states and presidents that are used in a matching game that focuses on primary and secondary stress. Students turn over the cards and read the names under the pictures, and then they must match the stress patterns of the vocabulary. For example, **Wa**shington and **Ke**nnedy match the stress pattern of three syllables with the first syllable stressed. This stress pattern can be designated by a long bar for the stressed syllable and dots for the reduced syllables: — ° ° (Grant, 2010). Additionally, students can list or group together those words that have the same stress pattern as demonstrated in Table 1.

VOCABULARY IN CONTEXT

The pronunciation of some words primarily depends on how they are used in context. For example, many words function as both nouns and verbs. Some have the same pronunciation, such as **_answer_**, but others change in word stress and vowel sounds depending on whether the word is used as a noun or a verb, such as *present* and *record*. Grant's (2010) textbook includes a list of two-syllable noun-verb pairs with and without stress shift. As students learn these word pairs and use them verbally, pronunciation is key to the distinction between the two parts of speech. The teacher can say a word and students can signify whether they heard the noun or the verb by holding up an index card that has *noun* written on one side and *verb* on the other. This response can also be done more discreetly with software such as LANschool (www.lanschool.com), ReLANpro (www.relanpro-usa.com), or Socrative (www.soc rative.com). Another exercise involves a student practicing saying a word in a pair or group while the partner or group members designate which part of speech is used. Afterward, they could create sentences using the words to share orally with the class.

HOMOPHONES AND WORDS COMMONLY CONFUSED

Homophones with the same sound present confusion for some students, as often evidenced in student writing that includes errors in using *there, their*, and *they're*. Thus, explaining how these homophones have the same pronunciation but different

Table 2 Model of Speaking Exercise Using Similar Words	
T: Name one **effect** of a poor economy on society. S1: A decrease in spending is one **effect**. S2: One **effect** is an increase in unemployment.	T: Explain one way a poor economy **affects** society. S1: A poor economy **affects** how people spend money. S2: People's jobs **are affected** by a poor economy.
T: What could you use **cloths** for? S1: I can use **cloths** to clean up a mess. S2: I use **cloths** to dust my furniture.	T: Describe your favorite **clothes**. S1: Faded blue jeans are my favorite **clothes** to wear. S2: My favorite **clothes** are blue like this blue shirt.

spellings and meanings can help students pay more attention to which word they actually want to use in their writing (also see Chapter 12). Additionally, students confuse some words that are somewhat similar in spelling and pronunciation, such as *effect-affect* and *cloths-clothes*. If students understand the different pronunciations and how spelling influences that pronunciation, then these words may be less confusing when they are writing them. An example exercise is a round robin conversation activity in which students respond to a teacher-generated prompt and use the highlighted word in their responses. Table 2 presents two pairs of prompts with student responses for each. This activity emphasizes both meaning and pronunciation. When students have exhausted their responses, a new prompt can be chosen.

WORD FORMS

Brown (1994) discusses techniques for learners to guess the meaning of vocabulary in context by which they analyze what they know about the prefixes, suffixes, and roots of the words. To use this technique, students must first learn the meanings of these words, and when doing this in class, wouldn't it also be beneficial to focus on how the affixes affect word stress? In English for academic purposes courses, students learn vocabulary from Coxhead's (2000) Academic Word List (AWL). As they learn these new words, they can expand their vocabulary by learning the additional word forms (which are available in the sublists maintained by Victoria University of Wellington, New Zealand, 2010). Students can note the stressed syllable and relate its sound to the color from the Color Vowel™ Chart and then use the words orally. An example of a speaking activity is using the vocabulary words in questions to be discussed and answered in groups. For example, after learning the word stress of AWL words, students could discuss teacher-generated questions that incorporate several words and then present their answers orally to the rest of the class. Students at higher levels could create questions, but these would need to be vetted by the teacher before completing the speaking activity. A variation of this activity can be used as a competitive review session in which student-generated questions are posed to teams by a group of student judges. The judges will determine if a response is accurate before awarding points to a team.

Here are a few examples of teacher-generated questions using words from Sublist 1:

- What are some **benefits** of **assessment**?

- What are some **factors** that **create** an **economic crisis**?

- What are some **significant issues** in the Washington, D.C., **area**?

As students learn any new word, they should also consider alternate forms of the word. One way to do this is to incorporate an activity to see what they know. For example, groups can list the word forms of selective vocabulary words and underline the word stress. For a more challenging exercise, they can designate any change in word stress and determine if there are any patterns in word stress. For instance, the following words have the same primary stress: *congra̱tulate, congra̱tulated, congra̱t-ulating,* but there is a change in stress for *congratula̱tion*. Another example is that *psycho̱logy* and *psycho̱logist* have the same primary stress, but *psycholo̱gical* and *psycho-lo̱gically* have a different primary stress from the first two words. Syllables before suffixes such as *–logy, –graphy,* and those beginning with *i* such as *–ion, –ical, –ically,* are stressed. Grant's (2010) textbook lists suffixes and the word stress guidelines associated with those suffixes. Taylor and Thompson (n.d.) advise, "when teaching word forms, draw students' attention to the color of the stressed syllable in one form of the word and compare it to the color of its related forms . . . *pho̱tograph* (ROSE) *photo̱grapher* (OLIVE) *photogra̱phic* (BLACK)" (p. 4).

Fill-in-the-blank vocabulary exercises focusing on meaning and parts of speech can also focus on pronunciation by orally checking the responses and emphasizing the changes in word stress. For additional pronunciation focus, students could stretch a rubber band on the stressed syllable as they say the correct term for the fill-in-the-blank exercise.

Please see Chapter 2 for more information and activities regarding word forms and AWL words. Chapter 8 also focuses on word forms regarding word stress in adjectives and adverbs.

Example: Write the word forms that exist for each word. Then use the correct word form in the sentences.

VERB	NOUN	ADJECTIVE	ADVERB
coordinate			
maintain			

1. Students need to _____ a good grade point average.
2. She is the _____ of the project, so you should contact her.
3. He has good hand-eye _____, so he plays sports well.
4. The swimming pool is closed in August for regular _____.
5. Let's _____ our efforts to get this resolved.
6. Her twins often wear _____ outfits.

Word Combinations

Lewis (2002) points out that vocabulary teaching that focuses on collocations or the co-text that often appears with the words being learned is more effective in language teaching than teaching the words out of context. Thus, learning phrasal verbs, collocations, and idiomatic expressions improves vocabulary knowledge. To expand and reinforce this knowledge for listening and speaking competence, pronunciation aspects related to these small thought groups should also be practiced. For example, stress of content words, reduction of function words, linking, and prominence should be examined when looking at the words as a whole group, especially if the typical word combinations are separated by other words. The pronunciation focus on these thought groups highlights the word combinations in meaningful contexts that facilitate long-term memory and practical use. The following subsections highlight activities and resources that incorporate pronunciation instruction with word combinations.

Poly Words and Phrasal Verbs

Lewis (2002) categorizes poly words as short phrases that have a meaning associated with the group of words, and these words are typically included in dictionaries. Some examples are *on the other hand*, *by the way*, *all at once*, and phrasal verbs such as *take over* and *put off*. As students learn these phrases or short thought groups, they should also learn the rhythm and linking of the phrase. For instance, with *all at once, all* and *once* are stressed words, but *all* would be longer and higher in pitch as the focus word. The word *at* is reduced to /ət/ instead of /æt/, and there is linking between *all* and *at*: /ɔlət/. Visual representations of the pronunciation should also be introduced. For example, the teacher can use larger letters for content words to focus on stress and smaller letters for reduced sounds and words. Additionally, linking of words can be represented with a line connecting the words, and the teacher can demonstrate how the words are said without linking and then with linking. These visual representations are very useful for lower levels since metalanguage discussions are difficult. Using these expressions in oral communication is the most beneficial practice. Cohen (2011) discusses how the repeated reading method and reader's theater could improve student fluency and rhythm. Dialogues that incorporate these common expressions could be orally read several times (Cohen recommends four times) to not only explore the vocabulary contextually but also improve on the pronunciation of these expressions.

The word stress of phrasal verbs such as *take out* and *drop off* is typically on the particle following the verb, but there are other pronunciation patterns. Hahn and Dickerson (1999) indicate that there are three patterns that are dependent on the particle used and the position of the verb: (1) stress the particle, as in *take **over***; (2) stress the verb, as in ***li***sten *to*; and (3) stress the first particle, as in *look **for**ward to*. When discussing some phrasal verbs, it is beneficial to also discuss the noun form and its stress, such as ***hand***out (noun) and *hand **out*** (verb). For meaningful practice of some phrasal verbs, the instructor can provide a list of phrasal verbs with the same verb and different particles, such as *take **out**, take **off***, and *take **in***. Students could record these words in sentences and emphasize in their pronunciation of the phrasal verbs that the particle is what distinguishes one phrase and its meaning from the others. Recorded sentences could be self-assessed for pronunciation and/or assessed by the instructor for pronunciation and meaning. Students at higher levels could practice by generating a story with a set of phrasal verbs. A different list could be given to each group and the stories shared with the class. Lists could be categorized by verb or stress pattern. Chapter 8 provides more information and activities regarding phrasal verbs.

Collocations

Collocations are sometimes included in dictionary definitions and/or can be searched in specific collocation dictionaries such as the *Oxford Collocation Dictionary Online for Advanced Learners* (n.d.). Alves, Berman, and Gonzales (2012) created the Word Combination Card, which provides key academic collocations related to high-frequency nouns and verbs, main points in writing (topic sentences and thesis statements), sentence starters, patterns of organization, and selected topics (e.g., business and finance, science and technology). As students use the collocation dictionary or the Word Combination Card to see what words are often associated with certain nouns and verbs, they can ascertain which words are emphasized and which are reduced. Additionally, they can determine which words can link together (e.g., *brief encounter* /bri **fin** kaʊn tər/, *close encounter* /kloʊ **sin** kaʊn tər/).

Lewis (2002) defines collocations as poly words that co-occur either through free, novel associations or fixed, institutionalized associations. Institutionalized collocations or common expressions include phrases such as *Sorry to interrupt, but could I just say . . .* and *Just a moment, please* (Lewis, 2002). Students can determine that *moment* is the focus word, and the vowel sound /oʊ/ (ROSE) is longer and higher in pitch. Additionally, they can determine that *just* and *a* are not only reduced but also linked together: /dʒəstə/. Institutionalized collocations could be introduced as targeted vocabulary that students are required to incorporate in their group discussion or speaking activity. Actually, many speaking textbooks already include targeted expressions for each unit. If students are learning how to use these expressions, then they should learn how to correctly pronounce them. This metacognitive focus on pronunciation should increase students' retention of the correct pronunciation more than just rote repetition.

Collocation pronunciation practice can reinforce how students verbally use various collocations for a word. For example, students can play a round robin game in groups or as a class. The group selects a word and one student needs to use a collocation with that word in a sentence. The next person uses the same word in a different collocation. Collocations can be provided or not, depending on whether students are practicing with newly learned vocabulary or reviewing what they should have already learned. This exercise focuses on meaning and pronunciation. In particular, the collocation would likely be uttered as one thought group that incorporates word stress of content words, linking between words, and emphasis on the focus word of the thought group. The teacher can monitor correct pronunciation and usage if the class is small or if the teacher works with one group at a time while the other groups of students are independently doing other tasks as part of a multi-group rotation activity. A review activity for higher levels includes dividing the class into two teams and one group of three judges. The teams can compete on how many collocations for a word they can come up with, and the judges would determine the correctness in usage and pronunciation.

Idiomatic Expressions
Idioms can be taught as thought groups with linking; for example, *cut it out* is pronounced as one thought group that is linked together so that it sounds like one word: /kʌtɪtaʊt/. Another example of linking ending consonants with vowels in the next

word is *a man of his word*: /ə mænəvɪz wɚd/. *A heart to heart talk* / ə hartə hartɔlk/ is another idiom that reduces function words with a schwa sound: *a* and *to*. However, the linking between the words is different because the ending sound of one word is the same sound as the initial sound of the next word, so /t/ is only pronounced once between the words. Typically, groups of idioms are taught by topic, so multiple idioms can be used by students to create short dialogues, stories, or lyrics, which can be marked for dividing thought groups with a slash mark (/) and designating words that can be linked in a thought group with a line between the words (_). Afterward, the student work can be shared orally with the class.

Conclusion

Teaching pronunciation in association with teaching vocabulary is essential for second language acquisition in terms of improving learners' speaking and listening skills and communicative competence. As students learn new words, they should learn the pronunciation of each word in addition to learning the definition(s) and spelling for each word. To facilitate this, pronunciation features should be taught to establish a foundation in understanding how a word or expression is pronounced. These features include guidelines for determining correct pronunciation of word stress, vowel and consonant sounds, thought groups, rhythm, and linking. The various activities and resources in this chapter are presented to provide some ways that pronunciation can be incorporated with vocabulary skills. Many of these activities can be used at varying degrees with children or adults as well as with different levels. Incorporating pronunciation activities such as those discussed in this chapter with vocabulary instruction provides a much richer learning experience for students and enhances their oral usage of words and expressions. To sum up, even though vocabulary may often be taught in association with reading, it is important that the oral use of the words be incorporated in the learning experience to improve oral/aural communication. Thus, learning guidelines for correct pronunciation provides second language learners with the tools to say words more accurately and fluently. To facilitate this, pronunciation-related posters such as Taylor and Thompson's Color Vowel™ Chart and accompanying student-generated word charts and/or Gilbert's (2008) Prosody Pyramid could be used as a visual reinforcement for students and quick references for teachers.

Resources

Bell, V., Cheney, J., King, P. J., & Moore, M. P. (2014). Words commonly confused. Santa Monica College. Retrieved from, http://homepage.smc.edu/reading_lab /words_commonly_confused.htm

Berman, M. (2008) The American English pronunciation card. Rockville, MD: Language Arts Press.

Diphthongs and triphthongs. (n.d.). Retrieved from http://www.yorku.ca/earmstro/ipa /diphthongs.html

English Vocabulary Exercises: GSL & AWL. (2014). Retrieved from http://www .englishvocabularyexercises.com/

English Vocabulary General Service List. (2014). Retrieved from http://www2.elc .polyu.edu.hk/CILL/generalServiceList.htm

References

Alves, M., Berman, M., & Gonzales, R. (2012). *The corpus-based word combination card: A writer's reference* (2nd ed.). Rockville, MD: Language Arts Press.

Brown, H. D. (1994). *Teaching by principles: An interactive approach to language pedagogy.* Upper Saddle River, NJ: Prentice Hall Regents.

Cohen, J. (2011). Building fluency through the repeated reading method. *English Teaching Forum, 3,* 20–27.

Coxhead, A. (2000). A new academic word list. *TESOL Quarterly, 34,* 213–238.

English Computerized Learning. (n.d.). *Products: Pronunciation Power 1 and 2.* Retrieved from http://www.englishlearning.com/products

Gilbert, J. B. (2008). *Teaching pronunciation: Using the prosody pyramid.* New York, NY: Cambridge University Press.

Grant, L. (2010). *Well said: Pronunciation for clear communication* (3rd ed.). Boston, MA: Heinle-Cengage Learning.

Hahn, L. D., & Dickerson, W. B. (1999). *Speechcraft: Discourse pronunciation for advanced learners.* Ann Arbor: University of Michigan Press.

Henry, L. (1999). *Pronunciation card games.* Brattleboro, VT: Pro Lingua Associates.

Lewis, M. (2002). *The lexical approach: The state of ELT and a way forward.* Boston, MA: Thomson-Heinle.

Mendez, E. (2010). How to set up oral homework: A case of limited technology. *English Teaching Forum, 3,* 10–19.

Oxford collocation dictionary online for advanced learners. (n.d.). Retrieved from http:// www.ozdic.com

Pearson Education. (2015). *ELLIS: A digital learning ELL curriculum.* Retrieved from http://www.pearsonschool.com/index.cfm?locator=PSZu72&PMDBSOLUTIONID =&PMDBSITEID=2781&PMDBCATEGORYID=&PMDBSUBSOLUTIONID =&PMDBSUBJECTAREAID=&PMDBSUBCATEGORYID=&PMDbProgramId=32507

Taylor, K., & Thompson, S. (n.d.). *Welcome to the color vowel chart*. Retrieved from http://americanenglish.state.gov/files/ae/resource_files/the_color_vowel_chart _teachers_guide.pdf

Taylor, K., & Thompson, S. (1999/2015). *The Color Vowel Chart*. Santa Fe, NM: English Language Training Solutions.

Victoria University of Wellington, New Zealand. (2010). *Sublist families of the Academic Word List*. Retrieved from http://www.victoria.ac.nz/lals/resources /academicwordlist/sublists

Anchoring Academic Vocabulary With a "Hard-Hitting" Haptic Pronunciation Teaching Technique

Michael Burri, Amanda Baker, and William Acton

his chapter describes a simple five-step haptic technique that enhances second language (L2) vocabulary development by more actively bringing in the pronunciation of the targeted words: the Rhythm Fight Club (RFC; Acton, n.d.). As the name suggests, the RFC involves a boxing-like movement that students typically find engaging and fun. The objective of the RFC is to support form-focused work on vocabulary and, at the same time, promote intelligible pronunciation. The RFC can also be modified and extended to L2 reading instruction in that systematic attention to pronunciation can contribute greatly to the encoding and learning process (Walter, 2008). In fact, the procedure can be applied in any teaching context, helping learners with new vocabulary, assisting with retaining meaning and usage as well as pronunciation. Both native- and nonnative-English-speaking instructors should find it useful and easy to work with.

Haptic Integration of English Pronunciation Teaching

Haptic integration is a new approach that makes systematic use of the kinesthetic and tactile senses or, in other words, movement and touch. The general framework is based on Essential Haptic-Integrated English Pronunciation (EHIEP; Acton, Baker, Burri, & Teaman, 2013; Teaman & Acton, 2013) and Acton-Haptic English Pronunciation System (Acton, n.d.), the haptic video version of EHIEP.

Literally, *haptic* means "relating to touch," or "grasp," from the Greek *haptikos*. Haptic technology (e.g., haptics) uses various technologies to give feedback to the user in the form of movement, pressure, and temperature. Today, we see haptic technology in smartphones (e.g., vibrations in tune with the phone ringing or in response to touching the screen), with video games (e.g., sensation of an engine revving in the hand controller), seats in 4D movie theatres that move with the action, and education (Minogue & Jones, 2006).

Haptic integration should help

- students learn and remember vocabulary and pronunciation better (Burri, 2014),

- instructors become more effective at providing in-class feedback on pronunciation,

- students become better at correcting their own pronunciation and embodying it in spontaneous speech (e.g., engaging in conversation outside the classroom).

There is a great deal of literature and research in the field of applied linguistics that attests to the positive impact and benefits of using gesture in language teaching and learning (e.g., Dahl & Ludvigsen, 2014; McCafferty, 2006). Morett (2014), for example, found that producing gestures (rather than viewing them) while speaking enhances the learning of foreign words, and Miller and Jones (Chapter 7 in this book) make a strong case for incorporating physical movement (e.g., gestures) to help integrate the learning and teaching of pronunciation and grammar. In related fields touch is widely utilized to bring together the senses for more focused learning. Haptic is generally referred to as the bonding or exploratory sense (Fredenbach, Boisferon, & Gentaz, 2009). Furthermore, touch enhances attention and concentration by managing emotional and visual distraction. Research suggests that, in some contexts, the physical touch (e.g., as a part of a quick hug) promotes that momentary "total focus" in less than 3 seconds (Nagy, 2011). Lastly, touch engages more of the entire body and brain in the process.

Haptic anchoring as used in this chapter, however, should be taken to mean using gesture plus touch to identify and anchor a feature of pronunciation. In the case of the RFC, this movement terminates or focuses on the stressed syllable in a word and/or word family. *Anchoring*, as we use the term, also indicates that a word is said out loud during a gesture. It is this multidimensional action (movement + touch + spoken word) that anchors not only the word, but its meaning and pronunciation in memory. Consequently, haptic pronunciation teaching can involve a number of gesture-based movements to

- differentiate between stressed and unstressed vowels,

- group and highlight prominent syllables,

- facilitate the learning of collocations (helping students remember what words go together, such as *get + up* and *sit + down*),

- emphasize word-level tone patterns or intonation.

The two specific applications that are explored in this chapter are (1) anchoring stress shift (as when a root form of a word becomes a different grammatical category, such as in **co**ntent and con**tent** or **stra**tegy and stra**te**gic) and (2) anchoring a word within its family, focusing on related words that share the same root form and meaning (see discussion of the Academic Word List later in the chapter). The RFC is used as a means to facilitate and deepen acquisition of new vocabulary, especially vocabulary encountered in academic course work and texts.

Vocabulary Work in Contemporary L2 Teaching

Nation (2006) provides a comprehensive overview of strategies and techniques for directed vocabulary work. In addition to paying attention to selected, key formal features of a new word and collocational relationships to other words, the meaning of a new vocabulary can be taught from several perspectives.

This specific focus on vocabulary naturally requires a focus on forms, requiring explicit teaching of different features such as spelling, morphology (e.g., identifying prefixes, word stem, and suffixes), and pronunciation (e.g., drilling and repeating a word's pronunciation). In terms of word usage, Nation (2006) suggests instructors identify the word class and examine its register and cultural connotations. He also outlines techniques such as using word cards, dictionaries, spelling dictation, and computer-based programs (e.g., lextutor.com) to work on collocations. In addition to Nation's practical suggestions, current theory on optimal instruction and acquisition of vocabulary proposes that it is generally best learned in context, using a more task-based approach (Nunan, 2004.)

This theory, however, has recently faced an interesting twist. File and Adams's (2010) work, for example, demonstrates that in some situations less contextualized vocabulary instruction may lead to an equal or even higher rate of retention than does more integrated instruction. Additionally, research examining and comparing the effectiveness of top-down (i.e., learning words in context) and bottom-up (i.e., learning words in isolation) approaches to academic vocabulary instruction to Chinese learners of English revealed that students in the bottom-up group slightly outperformed their peers in the top-down group in terms of "vocabulary size and controlled productive vocabulary knowledge" (Moskovsky, Jiang, Libert, & Fagan, 2014, p. 271). Such research partially vindicates more traditional, form-based practice that places emphasis on the use of word lists, grammar, synonyms and antonyms, and attention to derivational (prefixes and suffixes) forms and word-family association. Research suggests, in fact, that intermediate-level learners may benefit even more from paradigmatic, form-focused vocabulary work (Elgort & Warren, 2014). From a practical, teaching perspective, of course, being flexible enough to work with both word usage in context and a word's structural and semantic properties is ideal.

That framework serves as the conceptual basis of haptic-integrated vocabulary teaching in that a classroom-tested, haptic (movement + touch) pedagogical overlay and extension of File and Adams's (2010) principles can be applied in any setting (Acton et al., 2013). That may or may not include a relevant sentence or paragraph associated with a conversational or academic context. Rather, just the haptic-based technique outlined in this chapter is often very effective in anchoring vocabulary in general, thus creating a form of muscle memory. A key assumption is that a word can always be processed more experientially (haptically), in such a way as to better anchor (committing to memory) its meaning, pronunciation, structural, and "familial" properties.

Familial Connections: The Academic Word List Framework and Format

The word family (a set of words that share a common core meaning and form) used in this chapter (*valid*, *validity*, *validly*, *validate*, and *validation*) has been borrowed from the Academic Word List (AWL), which was developed by Coxhead (2000). The list was derived from a 3.5 million-word corpus and was designed to replace an earlier university word list. The source texts covered four main topic areas, each representing seven disciplines or subdisciplines, and source materials were journal articles, university textbooks, texts from selected corpora, and laboratory manuals.

The AWL and its derivatives now inform textbook development, dictionaries, and online vocabulary exercises. One of the advantages of drawing on the AWL is that it provides coverage of written undergraduate texts across a variety of disciplines to serve the vocabulary learning needs of a wide range of learners. In addition, the 10 sublists enable teachers to prioritize their attention with regard to vocabulary for materials development, activities, and assessment.

Focusing on pronunciation instruction, Murphy and Kandil (2004) use the AWL as a foundation for establishing which word stress patterns are the most frequent in English, revealing that 90% of the words in the AWL followed one of 14 patterns.[1] Among the five highest ranked were the 3-2, 2-2, 4-2, 2-1, and 4-3-1 patterns. In each of these sequences, the numbers, in order, refer to (1) number of syllables in the word; (2) the syllable with primary stress; and, for longer words, (3) the syllable with secondary stress. For example, the word *economic* is a 4-3-1 word, comprising four syllables with the third syllable containing primary stress and the first syllable housing the secondary stress. Haptic techniques such as the RFC can easily be mapped onto those patterns.

---

1 The RFC training as done in the Acton Haptic-Integrated English Pronunciation System includes attention to all 14 patterns (Acton, n.d.).

Anchoring all or most of the words in a word family aims to deepen the conceptual and grammatical—and physical—interconnections between the head word and related forms. That enhanced awareness of the other members of the word family and the core, shared meaning (as established through haptic technique use) seems to provide powerful support for learning vocabulary. Research by Macedonia and Klimesch (2014) has revealed that the combination of language and gesture has a positive impact on word retention, not only for short-term memory, but for long-term memory as well, especially in comparison with audiovisual stimuli alone. Furthermore, this research has made some preliminary connections to the role that emotion plays in language learning, suggesting that gesture, simultaneously coupled with heightened emotion, may further enhance the lexical anchoring. In the case of the RFC, the laughter and the overall enjoyment resulting from the execution of boxer-like punches in the classroom should serve as an additional emotional anchor, working in conjunction with physical anchoring established by the haptic technique.

Procedures for Haptic Anchoring of Academic Word List Vocabulary

In the model exercises that follow, we use the word *valid* as an example. We assume that it has been initially derived from a relevant academic text of some kind (e.g., spoken lecture; written text; word list of additional, associated, academic terms). The task is to embody, or rather haptically anchor and deepen, the experience of the term. This is done by involving its *family paradigm* so L2 learners can remember the word better.

Teacher Preparation

Before working on a reading text that contains words that are of high value, a teacher should prepare a graphic representation of the word family of the target word that students are expected to learn (see Chapters 1 and 8 for further discussion about word forms and pronunciation teaching). Consulting the AWL, it is relatively easy to locate and put into teachable form a word family. Table 1 is shown to students as a prereading task.

Typical usage of the family forms can be prepared by a teacher in advance, using, for example, one of the free dictionaries readily available online or the teacher's own imagination or experience. Possible example sentences may be something like the following:

- His opinion may be different than yours, but is equally **valid**.

- The evidence from the crime scene **validates** the investigator's theory.

Table 1 *Valid* Word Family Example

ACADEMIC WORD	WORD-LEVEL STRESS PATTERN[a]	DEFINITION[b]
Valid	2-1	(adj) legally or officially acceptable; based on what is logical or true
Validate	3-1-3	(verb) to prove that something is true; to make something legally acceptable
Validly	3-1	(adv) in a legally or officially acceptable manner
Validity	4-2	(noun) the state of being legally or officially acceptable; the state of being logical and true
Validation	4-3-1	(noun) to declare or make legally valid

[a] Patterns are based on Murphy and Kandil's (2004) identification of word-level stress patterns in the AWL.
[b] Definitions are based on those provided in the *Oxford Advanced American Dictionary for Learners of English: http://oaadonline.oxfordlearnersdictionaries.com*.

- The police questioned the **validity** of her argument, but later it was verified to be true.

- When children want **validation** for their decisions, they often turn to their parents for approval.

- The government confirmed that the company had **validly** purchased the property despite public protests to the contrary.

The purpose of providing students with the table, the exemplar sentences, and the haptic technique is to simultaneously anchor the pronunciation of the word with the learning of the word's meaning in a meaningful context. As is detailed below, although learners first practice the words haptically in isolation, they are then usually directed to practice them in a sentence, saying the entire sentence aloud and applying the haptic techniques to the key word.

Procedure of Rhythm Fight Club Technique
(see https://vimeo.com/61195605)

1. *Syllable awareness:* Identify the number of syllables in a word; for example, two syllables in *valid*: *va* ← *lid* (tap your thumb and middle finger together on each syllable).

2. *Word stress awareness:* Anchor the stressed syllable of the target word by moving your left hand across to touch your right hand on the stressed syllable. (Imagine that you are being slapped on your hand by your middle school teacher for mis-stressing the word!)

3. *RFC:* Hold something (e.g., tennis ball, stress ball, set of keys) in your right hand, and position your arm at a 90-degree angle. Drive your right arm forward with enthusiasm, as if punching something, to attend to the stressed syllable (*va*).

Important: Squeeze the ball or whatever is in the hand at the same time, and then go back, close to the body, to attend to the unstressed syllable (*lid*), by using very short jabs with your right hand. Repeat three or four times, being sure to use a sharp punching movement and strong squeeze.

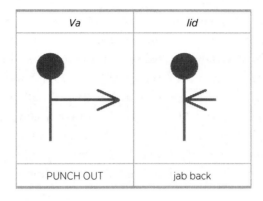

Va	*lid*
PUNCH OUT	jab back

4. *RFC with word family:* Repeat steps 1–3 for all words in the word family. Anchor each word haptically, focusing on the shift in stress positioning when relevant.

- **va**lidate
- **va**lidly
- va**li**dity
- vali**da**tion

5. *RFC in context:* Whenever possible, also anchor the target word haptically in the original text-context by going back to the text and saying the word in a phrase or short sentence while using the RFC. For example, "His opinion may be different than yours, but is equally valid." (Use RFC on last phrase only.)

6. (Optional) *RFC and sentence stress expansion:* Expand to use the RFC with other instances of prominent words in the sentence. In the example above, this could include both **different** and **va**lid: "His opinion may be **different** than yours, but is equally **va**lid."

For slower or less fluent speakers, the above example could include *opin*ion and *equal*ly in addition to **dif**ferent and **va**lid: "His o**pin**ion may be **dif**ferent than yours, but is **equal**ly **va**lid."

Each bolded syllable is punctuated by a sharp punching movement (while squeezing a ball or other instrument with the right hand). In the video model, the unstressed syllables in between are also represented by a series of short jabs, again with the right hand, but those additional movements are not essential to the impact of the RFC.

Breaking Down the RFC

The RFC is performed with hands in the starting position of a jab used in boxing and held at about diaphragm level. The right hand alternates on syllables with a forward or backward movement. On the stressed syllable of the phrase, the right hand does a strong forward punch. On an unstressed syllable, the right hand does either a small backward or forward jab. For example, in the sentence "That's very im**por**tant," you begin with a short jab forward (*That's*), followed by a backward movement (*ve–*), then another short jab forward (*–ry*) and another backward movement (*im–*). Then since the next syllable is stressed (*–**por**–*), you do a strong forward punch, making sure to simultaneously squeeze the ball, before ending with a final backward movement (*–tant*).

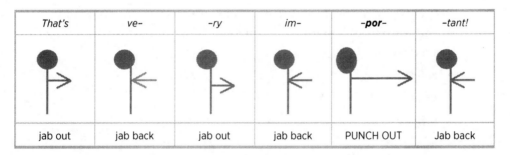

That's	ve-	-ry	im-	**-por-**	-tant!
jab out	jab back	jab out	jab back	PUNCH OUT	Jab back

The purpose of the RFC is to compact the syllables of speech, especially the unstressed syllables, creating a much more conversational "felt sense" for the learner. Thus each of the unstressed syllables, which are anchored to the short jabs or backward movements described above, are performed in quick succession. The stressed syllable, however, has a slightly longer duration that is emphasized by the strong punch forward. Especially for learners whose first language is characterized as more syllable-timed, this use of short jabs versus full strike helps to highlight the stress-timed nature of English.

Caveat emptor: The "fighting spirit" of this haptic protocol has to be kept in check to some extent, with not too much enthusiasm. That is done by carefully monitoring the execution of the jabs and punches. A jab should go either back to forward for about 10 centimeters, maximum. A punch, on the other hand, should go out to almost full extension of the arm.

For students or instructors with some degree of martial arts training, this strike can be even further accentuated by including hip movement. As you punch forward on the stressed syllable with your right hand, rotate the right hip forward sharply at the same time. This hip movement will give your technique a martial artist's feel, thus not only entertaining the class, but, more important, further anchoring the stress to the target word.

Instead of preparing a word family list, the steps above could also be applied in an integrated and spontaneous manner. For example, the teacher could use the procedure when a student encounters an unknown word during any language task.

Concluding Note

The RFC is not only effective; it is simply fun, and often wonderfully spontaneous and creative as well. Using the RFC requires little or no explicit training; you just have learners do the word with you. It is important to keep RFC anchoring haptic, that is, done with something that can be squeezed in the right hand to ensure that only the stressed syllable is anchored in the process. (Even a wadded up piece of paper works fine—as long as it is recycled at the end of the lesson, of course!)

Using the RFC in anchoring vocabulary or enhanced pronunciation is almost always met with an enthusiastic response from students. In working with academic vocabulary, particularly words that have very limited or highly esoteric contexts of usage, the impact of "taking off the gloves" and putting some "punch" behind the word and its lexical family is often striking—and memorable.

Resources

Haptic demo videos are available at http://www.actonhaptic.com/#!demos/c1yws
Bill Acton's blog on haptic pronunciation teaching and research is available at http://hipoeces.blogspot.ca

References

Acton, W. (n.d.). *HICPR: Haptic-integrated clinical pronunciation research and teaching.* Retrieved from http://hipoeces.blogspot.ca

Acton, W., Baker, A., Burri, M., & Teaman, B. (2013). Preliminaries to haptic-integrated pronunciation instruction. In J. Levis & K. LeVelle (Eds.), *Proceedings of the 4th Pronunciation in Second Language Learning and Teaching Conference* (pp. 234–244). Ames: Iowa State University.

Burri, M. (2014). Haptic-assisted vocabulary and pronunciation teaching technique. In A. Coxhead (Ed.), *New ways in teaching vocabulary* (2nd ed., pp. 189–191). Alexandria, VA: TESOL International Association.

Coxhead, A. (2000). A new academic word list. *TESOL Quarterly, 34*, 213–238.

Dahl, T., & Ludvigsen, S. (2014). How I see what you're saying: The role of gestures in native and foreign language listening comprehension. *Modern Language Journal, 98*, 813–833.

Elgort, I., & Warren, P. (2014). L2 vocabulary learning from reading: Explicit and tacit lexical knowledge and the role of learner and item variables. *Language Learning, 64*, 365–414.

File, K., & Adams, R. (2010). Should vocabulary be isolated or integrated? *TESOL Quarterly, 44*, 222–249.

Fredenbach, B., Boisferon, A., & Gentaz, E. (2009). Learning of arbitrary association between visual and auditory novel stimuli in adults: The "Bond effect" of haptic exploration. *PLoS ONE, 4*(3), e4844.

Macedonia, M., & Klimesch, W. (2014). Long-term effects of gestures on memory for foreign language words trained in the classroom. *Mind, Brain, and Education, 8*(2), 74–88.

McCafferty, S. G. (2006). Gesture and the materialization of second language prosody. *International Review of Applied Linguistics in Language Teaching, 44*, 197–209.

Minogue, J., & Jones, M. (2006). Haptics in education: Exploring an untapped sensory modality. *Review of Educational Research, 76*, 317–348.

Morett, L. (2014). When hands speak louder than words: The role of gesture in the communication, encoding, and recall of words in a novel second language. *Modern Language Journal, 98*, 834–853.

Moskovsky, C., Jiang, G., Libert, A., & Fagan, S. (2014). Bottom-up or top-down: English as a foreign language vocabulary instruction for Chinese university students. *TESOL Quarterly, 49*, 256–277.

Murphy, J., & Kandil, M. (2004). Word-level stress patterns in the academic word list. *System, 32*, 61–74.

Nagy, E. (2011). Sharing the moment: The duration of embraces in humans. *Journal of Ethology 29*, 389–393.

Nation, P. (2006). How large a vocabulary is needed for reading and listening? *Canadian Modern Language Review, 63*, 59–82.

Nunan, D. (2004). *Task-based language teaching*. Cambridge, England: Cambridge University Press.

Teaman, B., & Acton, W. (2013). Haptic (movement and touch for better) pronunciation. In N. Sonda & A. Krause (Eds.), *JALT 2012 Conference Proceedings* (pp. 402–409). Tokyo, Japan: JALT. Retrieved from http://jalt-publications.org/proceedings/articles/3285-haptic-movement-and-touch-better-pronunciation

Walter, C. (2008). Phonology in second language reading: Not an optional extra. *TESOL Quarterly, 42*, 455–474.

CHAPTER 3

Integrating Pronunciation Into Listening/Speaking Classes

Greta Muller Levis and John Levis

Years ago, when a friend came over to our house, we introduced him to our "daughter" at the time, who was sitting on the living room floor, with her back to the front door.

"Jim, this is our German exchange student, Monika. Monika, this is Jim."

"Hello," said Jim.

"Hello," replied Monika.

"You don't sound like you're from Germany," said Jim.

After Jim had left, Monika let us know how incredulous she was. "How did he know I didn't sound German? All I said was 'hello!'"

How indeed? The consonants /h/ and /l/ are not all that different in German than they are in English. The vowels /ɛ/ and /o/ are not necessarily very different either. What was it that made Jim think Monika sounded like she didn't have a foreign accent?

Probably it was a combination of things, including slight differences in vowel production, but more importantly, it was her prosody, or suprasegmentals, including the relative length (marked phonetically with a colon) and melody of the two syllables.

$$/h\,\varepsilon\,\text{-}\,l\,o^{\upsilon}\text{:}/$$

Prosody gives a language the characteristic shape that carries a person's meaning beyond the words being spoken. Jim heard in Monika's "hello" a person who was fluent and confident speaking English. Beyond the simple greeting word was an expression of her ability to communicate in a familiar and comfortable way.

Our Goals

In this chapter, we have several goals. First, we want to show you that explicit attention to suprasegmentals is essential to teaching spoken communication. We also want to explain why two suprasegmentals, prominence and final intonation, are particularly useful in English. In addition, we want to give you some ideas of how prominence and final intonation can be integrated into a listening/speaking class.

Pronunciation defines the ways a person speaks English, through both segmentals (the vowel and consonant sounds) and suprasegmentals (word stress, rhythm, prominence, and intonation). Two suprasegmentals in particular, prominence and final intonation, are very important. Prominence is the major emphasis given to a word or syllable in a phrase or sentence. Hahn (2004) did an experiment with one lecture spoken in three different ways by the same native Korean speaker: with correct sentence prominence, incorrect prominence, and zero prominence. Listeners understood the lecture much better with correct prominence, even with the same speaker and the same content.

Final intonation is the way the voice pitch moves after the prominent vowel to the end of a phrase. In English, this usually means the voice pitch goes up (rising intonation) or down (falling), a combination of the two (falling-rising), or stays flat (level). Pickering (2002) analyzed the way a native-Korean-speaking teacher, who was understandable but difficult to follow, used intonation while teaching. She found that he used much more frequent falling intonation than an American teaching a similar class.

We want to give you some ideas of how prominence and final intonation can be integrated into teaching oral communication. They add meaning beyond the words alone; learners need to understand that meaning. We hope you and your students will be able to take these ideas and expand them in many speaking and listening contexts.

Prominence and Final Intonation:
Two Essential Suprasegmentals

Prominence is the use of pitch and syllable length to call attention to a word or syllable in a phrase. *Final intonation* is the way the voice moves after the pitch jump of the prominent syllable. Both work together in the English intonation system, but each communicates its own meanings. It is good to separate them in teaching so that students can clearly learn both elements of the system. (Chapters 4, 5, and 6 also discuss ways to teach prominence.)

In dialogues in this chapter, prominence is marked in CAPITAL LETTERS and final intonation is marked with arrows. Notice where the prominent syllables are in Dialogue 1 and what happens with the intonation following the prominent syllable.

Dialogue 1

John: I thought we could go to the LIbrary. ↘
Greta: To work on our PAper? ↗
          I'd rather go to a COFfee shop. ↘
John: Mmm NICE. ↘

Teaching Prosody

Knowing the general system of prominence and final intonation will help you teach these elements without getting yourself in trouble. The better you understand the system, the easier it will be for you to plan and explain.

Prominence

1. The prominent syllable in a phrase is the stressed syllable of the last content word (noun, verb, or adjective) in the phrase. *The last content word is always the prominent syllable* unless there is a very good reason to do something different.

2. Prominence belongs on the main stressed syllable of a word (e.g., *LIbrary, PAper*) or a word construction such as a compound noun (e.g., *COFfee shop*).

3. The prominent syllable is longer in duration (more than two times longer) than other stressed syllables.

4. The prominent syllable usually has an abrupt change in pitch, often to a higher level.

5. When there are no content words, prominence goes on the last function word in a phrase. But it normally does not go on pronouns. In Dialogue 2a, Monika paces prominence on the function word *are* since there are no content words. This is normal prominence.

Dialogue 2a

Monika: HI, Jim. ↘ How ARE you? ↘
Jim: FINE. ↘

6. There are special circumstances where prominence rules are adjusted. For example, if two people ask each other the same question, the word that is prominent may change for the second speaker. In Dialogue 2b, Monika uses the normal prominence in the question "How ARE you?" but Jim changes the prominence to return the question to "How are YOU?" In doing so, he changes the prominent word to YOU, almost as if he were physically handing the question back.

Dialogue 2b

Monika: HI, Jim. ↘ How ARE you? ↘
Jim: FINE. ↘ How are YOU? ↘

7. Another special circumstance that requires prominence on a word that is not the last content word is when the last content word has recently been said. For example, in Dialogue 2c, Monika asks Jim whether he's spent time in Germany. Germany becomes old information, so when Jim responds, he must make the new information ("southern") prominent and de-emphasize the old information ("Germany"; see also Chapters 5 and 7).

Dialogue 2c

Monika: HI, Jim. ↘ How ARE you? ↘
Jim: FINE. ↘
             How are YOU? ↘
Monika: I'm GOOD. ↘ So have you ever gone to GERmany? ↗
Jim: YES, actually. ↘ Last SUMmer. ↘
             I spent time in SOUTHern Germany. ↘

Final Intonation

8. Almost any grammatical structure can have either rising or falling intonation after the pitch change of prominence. Intonation is a choice that equates more with a speaker's level of certainty. In general, falling intonation indicates that the speaker is more certain; rising intonation indicates that the speaker is not yet finished or is uncertain about something. (For more on teaching final intonation, see the Chapters 8 and 9.)

9. Generally, statements are said with falling intonation. Likewise, *Wh–* (or information) questions are usually said with falling intonation (e.g., "How ARE you?" ↘ in Dialogue 2).

10. Some phrases are parenthetical in nature. That is, they add information that is not crucial to the understanding of the phrase. These phrases often are said with a low, flat intonation, possibly ending with a slight rise. One example from Dialogue 2 is *Jim* in "HI, Jim." ➔ Notice how different this is than if someone were actually calling out to Jim with two prominent words and falling intonation in "HI! ↘ JIM!" ↘

Teaching Prosody as Part of Speaking

When teaching prosody, you need a variety of practice types. In the activities in this chapter, we give ideas for exercises that involve focused listening, individual and choral mimicry of a teacher or recording, reading dialogues aloud, and production of students' own language. In all cases, teachers should focus the activity by telling students what particular aspect of pronunciation they are trying for. Then, when you listen to students individually, give feedback only on that target.

Choral mimicry is a particularly powerful tool because students get a lot of practice in a relatively short amount of time, and it is less intimidating than having to speak individually. Choral mimicry can happen either as a response to a teacher or at the same time as the teacher. In either case it has the power to develop prosodic memory in the same way that singing in a choir helps singers develop musical memory (see also Chapter 7).

Pronunciation practice involves both mental and physical learning, and it also affects students' identities. Some parts of prosody can sound weird, funny, or bad to different students because it is so different from what they are used to. We recommend being aware of this by allowing students to "hide" in the choral crowd as they practice new things, by giving clear and gentle corrections, and by being sensitive to students' discomfort.

Teaching Length

We urge you to teach length separately from pitch when you introduce prominence. We begin with length because it is easier for students to hear and practice and for teachers to explain than pitch movement. It is very helpful to have students embody the stretched-out vowels in stressed syllables. This can be done by having them stretch a rubber band as they say the stressed vowel. Other physical embodiment of length can include students moving a hand sideways as they say the stressed syllable or tossing a soft ball underhand to themselves or another student as they stretch out the stressed vowel (see also Chapter 2).

Be sure that students move the rubber band, hand, or ball at exactly the same time as they stretch out the stressed vowel. The idea is to match the physical feeling in their bodies with the physical feeling in their mouths.

Teaching Pitch

The up or down pitch change of prominence can be easily confused with final intonation, which is the rising or falling of pitch *following* the pitch change. The pitch change of prominence is generally an abrupt jump up or down. The vowel is lengthened during the pitch change.

The pitch movement *after* this abrupt jump can be a falling or rising slide (if the prominent syllable is the last syllable of the phrase, as in *NONE*). Or it can be a step down or up (if the prominent syllable is not the final syllable of the phrase, as in *NEver*).

To teach these two pitch movements, demonstrate for students how to trace the pitch with their hands. You can also draw the pitch movement over a phrase on the board and then say the phrase to demonstrate. Ask students to trace the pitch movement as you say the phrase. Then ask them to hum the pitch movement quietly while you say the phrase, encouraging them to continue the hand trace. Finally, ask them to say the phrase quietly while you say it as well.

Activity Types: Controlled, Bridging, Communicative

Pronunciation activities run the gamut, from very controlled (allowing maximum attention to language form) to very uncontrolled (allowing maximum attention to communicating meaning). Mimicry is generally a very controlled activity. Free speech can be very communicative, but a teacher lacks control over the outcome.

Teaching pronunciation as part of oral communication, however, needs more than controlled and communicative activities. It needs a broad category in the middle that allows learners to pay attention to both form and meaning. We call these *bridging activities*; they are a bridge from controlled to communicative. Pronunciation learners need lots of controlled practice to make new pronunciation patterns feel and sound normal. They also need speaking practice where the pronunciation point is essential to communicative success.

Controlled, bridging, and communicative activities are important in teaching pronunciation, and all three have a place in integrating pronunciation into the teaching of speaking. In learning some types of functional expressions, controlled mimicry and reading are important to begin to create a prosodic memory of what the phrase should sound like. Once there is some measure of control, learners need to start making the language their own while still thinking about pronunciation. This is the realm of bridging activities. Finally, it is important to have practice that is fully meaning-oriented, or communicative.

In our example activities, we suggest controlled, bridging, and communicative activities for each topic: greetings, small talk, rejoinders, and repetition. From these examples, we encourage you to develop your own activities.

Greetings and Small Talk: What You Need To Know

Greeting routines and small talk are a great place to introduce suprasegmentals, especially prominence. Greetings are often taught the first day of a course. They can be addressed in increasingly complex ways for beginners to intermediate to advanced learners. They are relatively frozen in the words, structures, questions, and answers that are used, so students will have many opportunities to practice them both in and out of the classroom, depending on the context of instruction. In addition, success in greeting routines is a great entree into a continuing conversation, giving students further opportunities for speaking practice.

The simplest greeting routine consists simply of "Hello."

> *Dialogue 3*
>
> Jim: Hello. ↘
> Monika: Hello. ↘

This dialogue is a good introduction to English prominence since it gives students a chance to practice a longer prominent stressed syllable in "helLO."

A variant of "hello" can be introduced, and names can be added to the dialogue. The language addition is simple, but the prosodic change is somewhat complex. Adding names modifies the melodic contour.

> *Dialogue 4*
>
> Jim: Hello, ↘ Monika. →
> Monika: Hi, ↘ Jim. →

This conversation now also uses parenthetical prosody. The names are not prominent and are pronounced with parenthetical intonation.

Another variation to this simple routine is to add small talk questions, such as "How are you?" or "How's it going?" Further questions usually include a variety of safe topics (such as the weather or origins), but almost always both people ask each other the same questions.

Dialogue 5

Jim:	HI, Monika.
Monika:	HelLO, Jim. <u>How ARE you?</u> ↘
Jim:	I'm FINE. <u>How are YOU?</u> ↘
Monika:	I'm GOOD, thanks. <u>So where are you FROM?</u> ↘
Jim:	New YORK. <u>Where are YOU from?</u> ↘
Monika:	FRANKfurt.

When teaching the pronunciation of greetings and small talk, remember that greetings almost always use normal prominence. Small talk questions may put prominence on unusual words when the questions are repeated.

Teaching Greetings and Small Talk

We have found that teaching greetings and the stress of names in the first day or week of class is a great way to get students to practice putting prominence on the last word in a phrase. Getting to know each other's names is a fairly common introductory activity to a class. And from the point of view of pronunciation, practicing names helps students practice the length of the prominent syllable in relatively invariant phrases.

We have included a sequence of controlled, bridging, and communicative activities for both greetings and small talk. While you can pick and adapt from these activities, we recommend that you generally follow this basic sequence. Changing pronunciation is difficult and requires a lot of focused concentration. It helps to use very controlled contexts at first and to gradually wean students from that control before asking them to produce the new pronunciation at the same time as they communicate real messages.

The following sequence of exercises can be adapted for most levels of classes other than very low beginners. Although the "How ARE you/How are YOU" repeated questions may be straightforward for beginners, some other small talk activities may not be appropriate for low-proficiency students. Note that the explanations written here are long, but the activities and explanations should be taught at a relatively quick pace.

Greetings and Names

CONTROLLED ACTIVITY	COMMENTS
1. Walk around the room introducing yourself. There is no instruction or correction at this point. Let all students introduce themselves. Teacher: Hi. My name's John LEvis. What's YOUR name? Student: I'm _____. 2. Write your self-introduction on the board and ask students to listen for the most prominent, or stressed, word. You should say the phrase as often as needed at a normal pace. Board/Teacher: I'm Greta Muller Levis. 3. Have students choose names to say in the dialogue while they are doing something physical. A: Hel**LO**. My name's _____ _____. B: **HI**. I'm _____ _____.	Once students have identified the last name as prominent, underline it and ask students to listen for what makes that name sound prominent. Students will usually identify length, pitch, and/or loudness. All are correct, but we recommend concentrating on length. *Adaptations* 1. Do choral mimicry with the names. 2. Half the class can be A, and the other half B, for choral production of the dialogue. 3. Pairs do the dialogue.

Women's names	*Men's names*
Sue Baker	Tom Wilson
Mary Johnson	Jim Anderson
Jade Chang	David Smith
Maria Sanchez	Steven Jones
Monika Sand	Carlos Silva

BRIDGING ACTIVITY	COMMENTS
Have two students, Student A and Student B, who are next to each other, introduce themselves with this dialogue: A: Hel**lo**. My name's _____ _____. B: **Hi**. I'm _____ _____. Student B then turns to the person on the other side and has the same conversation: B: Hel**lo**. My name's _____ _____. C: **Hi**. I'm _____ _____. Student C continues with Student D and so on around the class. The last student has the final conversation with Student A.	A simple activity for the first or second day of class is a chain exercise. It is mechanical in that it is much the same routine for each student, but it is communicative in that students are actually introducing themselves. Adapt for advanced students with the addition of small talk (e.g., "Nice to meet you") and peer introductions. Personal names are one of the most challenging uses of prominence for many students. Students may not like their names with English prominence. Encourage laughter and light-heartedness, and be gentle in correction. Tell students that *they* decide which syllable of their name is stressed.

YOU Prominence in Small Talk

CONTROLLED ACTIVITY	COMMENTS

1. Tell students to listen to the sentences and underline the prominent word.
 	
   a. What have you been doing?
 	
   b. What kind of food is your favorite?
 	
   c. Did you go on vacation last summer?
 	
   d. When are you leaving?
 	
   e. Do you have a car?
 	
   f. What's your favorite movie?
 	
2. Tell students to listen to the sentences again. Ask them, "Can the sentence can begin a conversation?"
	You can read sentences aloud or record them. Any of these questions can have prominence on the last content word or on *you/your*. If the prominence is on *you/your*, it means the question was already asked once in the conversation. Mix prominence placement between the last word and *you/your*.
	
	Examples
	
	What have you been DOing? (The answer to the question, "Can the sentence begin a conversation?" is yes.)
	
	What kind of food is YOUR favorite? (The answer to the question, "Can the sentence begin a conversation?" is no.)

BRIDGING ACTIVITY	COMMENTS

Tell student pairs to have a conversation using one of the partial conversations. Tell them to fill in the correct information for themselves and to be sure to repeat any questions that have the word *you* in them.
 	
A: Hi. It's good to see you again. How ARE you?
 	
B: I'm doing pretty good. How are YOU?
 	
A: _____.
 	
B: _____.
 	
And so on.
 	
A: Hi, _____. What have you been DOing?
 	
B: I have a new job. It keeps me busy!
 	
   What have YOU been doing?/What about YOU?
 	
A: _____.
 	
B: _____.
 	
And so on.
 	
A: So did you like the movie?
 	
B: It wasn't too bad. But I didn't like the acting much.
 	
   _____?
 	
A: _____.
 	
And so on.
	This activity includes controlled language and opportunities for learners to add their own language and ideas. This makes it more challenging for them to concentrate just on pronunciation.
	
	Sometimes we repeat questions with a generic question: *What about YOU?* or *How about YOU?*
	
	This exercise encourages learners to keep a conversation going. This can be challenging for many learners who are used to simply reading dialogues.

Greetings and Small Talk (Speed Friending)	
COMMUNICATIVE ACTIVITY	**COMMENTS**
	This activity calls for fluent question asking and repeating questions with a changed sentence prominence. As written, it is not appropriate for beginners.
	Discussing speed friending before starting the activity may help activate a schema.

Situation: Students write down five to eight yes/no or *Wh-* questions they think are important to find out about someone else. All students sit on two sides of a table, facing one other student.

Tell students that they will meet many different people in a short time and will have only 3 minutes to talk to each one. Ask each other questions to find out information that is of interest. If they ask you a question, you can ask it back with changed prominence on YOU.

Ask students to take notes about things you have in common with the other person and what you find most interesting about them

Then move on to the next person and repeat your speed friendship questions. Evaluate each person as a potential friend.

When to Use Rising Intonation

Many teachers and students believe that all questions in English are spoken with rising intonation. This is not true. All questions and statements can be, and are, spoken with rising or falling intonation (see Table 1). Speakers' choice of rising or falling depends on what they want to communicate. Remember that final intonation is the movement of the pitch after the pitch change of prominence.

Table 1	Grammar and Intonation in English	
GRAMMAR	RISING INTONATION EXAMPLE	FALLING INTONATION EXAMPLE
Yes/no questions	*Did you find some money?*↗ (Meaning: polite)	*Did you find some money?*↘ (Meaning: businesslike)[a]
Statements	*I found some money.*↗ (Meaning: surprise)	*I found some money.*↘ (Meaning: assertion)
Wh– questions	*WHERE did you find some money?*↗ (Meaning: repeat)	*Where did you find some MOney?*↘ (Meaning: neutral asking for information)

[a] These terms come from Thompson (1995).

Yes/No Questions

Yes/No questions can be spoken with rising or falling intonation. This does not give them a special meaning. Their meaning changes slightly, perhaps from more polite to more businesslike, but these small differences in meaning do not affect their general function. In contrast, statements and *Wh–* questions show much greater changes in meaning when spoken with rising or falling intonation. As a result, the following activities focus on intonation changes for statements and *Wh–* questions, but not for yes/no questions.

Statements/Phrases With Rising Intonation: What You Should Know

Dialogue 6 is between an adult daughter and her father talking on the phone in the middle of the day.

> *Dialogue 6*
>
> Daughter: Guess what? ↘ Someone hit my car today. ↘
> Father: *Really?* ↗ *Someone hit your car?* ↗
> Daughter: A driving student and instructor. ↘ They left their name and insurance. ↘

This dialogue highlights the generalizations about statements in Table 1. The daughter expresses an assertion about her car getting hit. The father's repetition of her statement uses rising intonation, which gives the statement a special meaning of surprise.

Wh– Questions With Rising Intonation: What You Should Know

The normal intonation for *Wh–* questions is falling. But sometimes *Wh–* questions have rising intonation and a special placement of sentence focus. There are several important differences between normal and special *Wh–* questions. Normal *Wh–*

questions have prominence at the end of the sentence and fall in pitch after the prominent word.

Examples: Where are you GOing? ↘   How's the WEAther? ↘

Wh– questions with rising intonation are special. They can have special grammar ("You went WHERE?"), and they always have prominence on the *Wh–* word. The intonation after the prominent word rises. They ask for repetition, either because the listener didn't hear specific information clearly or because the listener heard it but didn't believe it.

Examples: WHERE are you going? ↗   You're going WHERE? ↗

Rising Intonation on Statements

The next three activities show how the same idea can be used in controlled, bridging, and communicative ways. They recycle both the language function (expressing surprise) and the pronunciation topic (rising intonation on statements).

Surprising Statements!	
CONTROLLED ACTIVITY	**COMMENTS**
Have student A draw a surprising statement from the collection and says it aloud with feeling. Student B responds with a similar statement with rising intonation to express surprise.	*Materials*
	10-12 slips of paper, each with a statement that a student can say to the class with a preface (e.g., Guess what? ↘ Oh, no! ↘)
Example Statements and Rejoinders	
A: Guess what? ↘ This morning my toilet overflowed. ↘	*Sample statements*
B: You're kidding! ↘ Your toilet overflowed? ↗	Cool! School is canceled tomorrow.
A: I don't believe it. ↘ I failed my test. ↘	I can't believe it! The rent is going up by $100.
B: Really?↗ You failed your test? ↗	
A: Oh, no! It's going to snow a lot. ↘	You'll be happy. I finally took out the trash.
B: _____?	

continued

BRIDGING ACTIVITY	COMMENTS
Have students brainstorm their own surprising statements, which are then listed for all to see. Student A chooses one statement at random, and Student B has to come up with a rejoinder. In each rejoinder, students should repeat the statement as closely as possible and use rising intonation.	This is a bridging activity because students pay attention to more than just pronunciation. The statements are known to everyone, but a student's choice is not, nor is the rejoinder. *Adaptations* 1. Students can each write two surprising statements. 2. Pairs can write surprising statements together. 3. The class can brainstorm statements 4. Practice in pairs. 5. Practice as a class, calling on different student pairs.
COMMUNICATIVE ACTIVITY	**COMMENTS**
1. Teacher provides a surprising statement about their life. Students (either voluntarily or assigned) provide a rejoinder. 2. Ask the class a question such as "What was the most surprising thing that happened to you this weekend?" Teacher responds with a rejoinder. 3. Students ask each other the question in #2 and respond to each other.	These ideas are for later classes and allow recycling of the target language use in real communication. This builds on what often happens in classes, in which teachers and students chat before class. In this activity, the chat is targeted toward what was taught in rising intonation on statements.

The next three activities are for rising intonation on *Wh–* questions. Instead of all following the same topic, as in the surprising statements activities, these show how controlled, bridging, and communicative activities can have the same pronunciation feature in focus but use different topics to achieve goals.

Practicing Special *Wh-* Questions

CONTROLLED ACTIVITY	COMMENTS
Have students practice the following conversations. Use the intonation as marked. For normal *Wh-* questions, use falling intonation. For special *Wh-* questions, put focus on the *Wh-* word and let your voice rise to the end of the question.	Special *Wh-* questions never start a conversation, so it's important to give students a context for the questions.
A: Do you have plans for this summer? ↘	The activity is controlled because it provides all the language and the intended intonation.
B: I'm going to Paris.	
A: You're going WHERE? ↗	Pairs can practice more by switching roles.
B: Paris. I'm visiting my sister.	
A: I need to find a new place to live.	
B: What's wrong with where you are now?	
A: It has ants everywhere.	
B: What does it have?	
A: Ants. Little bugs that are all over.	
B: Gross.	

BRIDGING ACTIVITY	COMMENTS
Tell students to look only at their own parts of the conversation. Student A starts the conversation. Student B chooses a response. Student A responds appropriately.	This is a branching conversation. It is a kind of controlled information gap built around limited responses that the other person does not know.
A: I'm studying in China next year.	
B: WHERE are you going? ↗ WHEN are you going? ↗	In this type of dialogue, Student A reads the first statement. Student B then has a choice of reading the WHERE or WHEN question. Student A responds with the appropriate answer from the two choices. Student B then responds appropriately, and so on.
A: China. It's really exciting. Next year. In February.	
B: Wow. That's around Chinese New Year. Cool. I was there 5 years ago.	
A: Is that when they give kids red envelopes? WHEN were you there? ↗	Like any information gap, students can have their responses on separate pieces of paper, or they can have one piece of paper where they cover up the left or right half so they cannot see what the other person might say.
B: Yeah. Kids love that holiday. 5 years ago.	

continued

Practicing Special Wh– *Questions, continued*

COMMUNICATIVE ACTIVITY	COMMENTS
Have students draw five to seven designs or shapes on a piece of paper. *Do not show your drawing to your partner.* Sit back to back or side by side so you can't see your partner's paper. Describe your picture so your partner can draw it. Your partner should ask questions for clarification and repetition.	This is a common type of activity in which students describe a drawing. The partner has to reproduce the drawing by asking questions for clarification.
A: OK. In the top left corner, there's a star. It has five points.	Like all communicative activities, students have a lot of freedom in the language they choose. The use of special *Wh–* questions is modeled but cannot be required. Rising statements are also very likely.
B: A star. WHERE is it? ↗	
A: In the top left. And there's a square on the top right.	
B: WHAT'S on the right? ↗	
A: A square. Are you ready for more?	
Game continues until finished, then students switch roles.	

Conclusion

The explanations and activities in this chapter should help you create pronunciation activities that integrate with the speaking activities you already use in your classes. Because pronunciation presents unique challenges, we encourage you to provide controlled and bridging pronunciation practice before asking students to take on the extra load of communicative activities that also target pronunciation. Pronunciation should be integrated with speaking, but integrating it takes some care so that students can successfully learn pronunciation and speaking together.

References

Hahn, L. D. (2004). Primary stress and intelligibility: Research to motivate the teaching of suprasegmentals. *TESOL Quarterly, 38,* 201–223.

Pickering, L. (2002). The role of tone choice in improving ITA communication in the classroom. *TESOL Quarterly, 35,* 233–255.

Thompson, S. (1995). Teaching intonation on questions. *ELT Journal, 49,* 235–243.

CHAPTER 4

Integrating Pronunciation With Presentation Skills

Veronica G. Sardegna, Fu-Hao William Chiang, and Mimi Ghosh

Since the late 1980s, practitioners and researchers have been advocating linking pronunciation with communicative activities and suggesting ways in which pronunciation skills could be taught alongside oral communication skills (Levis & Grant, 2003; Murphy, 1991). In practice, however, most language textbooks continue to lag behind these efforts (Watts & Huensch, 2013). This problem is exacerbated by the fact that teachers often lack the necessary training in phonology and pronunciation teaching (Derwing & Munro, 2005; Murphy, 2014) that could potentially help them bridge the lack of integration in language textbooks and/or help them address the diverse needs of their learners. In fact, reports in the literature suggest that it is most probably because of lack of teacher training and knowledge in pronunciation that teachers find it difficult to achieve an appropriate balance between pronunciation and speaking skills (Levis & Grant, 2003). To address these concerns, this chapter proposes a balanced approach to teaching pronunciation and presentation skills that is grounded in second language acquisition theory and English phonological learning. The approach is based on the following pedagogical assumptions:

1. A natural and reciprocal interdependence exists between the oral processes of speaking, listening, and pronunciation for the development of oral language proficiency (Murphy, 1991).

2. Pronunciation improvement takes a considerable amount of time and effort (Murphy, 1991) and does not primarily occur in the classroom. It depends largely on students taking control of their own learning by engaging in self-teaching and self-monitoring practice activities outside of class (Sardegna, 2011, 2012).

3. Learner empowerment through strategy training facilitates and increases the chances of pronunciation improvement and assists learners in their self-regulated efforts during oral practice (Sardegna, 2011, 2012; Sardegna & McGregor, 2013).

4. Learner empowerment is enhanced through a pedagogy for learner autonomy (Jiménez Raya, 2011). Under this pedagogical framework, the teacher provides resources and explicit knowledge of skills and strategies; encourages responsibility, choice, and flexible control; promotes critical reflection and self-directed learning; and provides opportunities for self-assessment and awareness-raising.

The chapter is organized in three sections. First, it provides an overview of the connections between pronunciation and presentation skills and offers project ideas and suggestions for integrating the two skills. Second, it focuses on one pronunciation feature—prominence—and discusses why and how it can be taught, practiced, and improved while preparing for an oral presentation. Finally, it offers pedagogical suggestions and sample slides that can be used for practice.

The Connections Between Pronunciation and Presentation Skills

A major objective of presenting before an audience is communicating ideas by speaking clearly and intelligibly. In other words, it is crucial that the speech is delivered in a manner whereby the audience can understand its intended meaning. As repeatedly argued in the literature, the goal for successful oral communication should be intelligible (rather than native-like) speech (Derwing & Munro, 2005, 2014; Levis, 2005), thereby giving focal attention to those features that affect speech intelligibility the most. Although research on intelligibility issues is still in its infancy, a number of studies have underscored the importance of stress to intelligibility at the word level and at the phrase level (Hahn, 2004; Zielinski, 2008). Often, oral presentations require presenters to relay different types of information (e.g., lists, comparisons, contradictory statements, requests). Assigning stress to the wrong syllable or word when providing these types of information may confuse the audience or require a longer processing time, which generally frustrates the listener. In fact, the prosodic realization of a word greatly influences the way its meaning is integrated into discourse (Cutler, Oahan, & van Donselaar, 1997). Undeniably, "stress is a good candidate for prioritization" (Derwing & Munro, 2014, p. 48) in the language classroom. Segmental priorities (i.e., consonant and vowel sounds) based on the functional load principle have also been empirically validated (see Munro & Derwing, 2006). Yet more studies supporting the relevance of this principle in multicultural contexts are still needed.

Furthermore, an oral presentation is a task that many teachers frequently assign

English language learners (ELLs) and that many ELLs are expected to master in academia and the workplace. These facts make oral presentations not only a task that is appropriate for any ELL at any age or stage of learning, but also a task that can be meaningful, authentic, and useful for ELLs around the world. A meaningful and authentic project can also increase learners' motivations to work on that project (for project ideas, see Table 1). Generally, the more meaningful and useful the topic is perceived to be, the more likely students will put more time and effort into preparing their oral presentations. As discussed earlier, for students to improve their pronunciation skills, it is critical that they devote a considerable amount of time and effort to private practice. The important role of planned (versus unplanned) discourse for achieving successful oral communication has also been highlighted (Williams, 1992). If students have time to prepare and practice a script, they can focus on improving their pronunciation skills and oral techniques as part of their preparation. Therefore, the selection of a good topic for students' oral presentations is paramount. Teachers should perhaps allow flexibility in the choice of topic to the extent possible in order to increase student engagement and maximize rehearsal time on task. After all, flexible control is a step toward increased learner autonomy (Jiménez Raya, 2011).

Apart from intelligible speech and a good project idea, two other integral components of a successful oral presentation are clear guidelines regarding expectations for the various phases of the project (preparation, practice, oral presentation) and good organization for the presentation. The clearer the expectations, the more likely students will stay focused and present a successful product. Also, as clearly stated by

Table 1 Project Ideas	
FOR LOWER LEVEL ELLS	**FOR HIGHER LEVEL ELLS**
• Choose a favorite animal from your local zoo. Research the animal and present your findings.	• Compare your native culture with your second language culture and present your findings.
• Survey your classmates, a grandparent, or a friend on topics related to family, hobbies, culture, and favorite things, and present your findings.	• Do a verbal book report on two books by the same author (or two paintings by the same artist, two songs by the same singer, etc.). Discuss the similarities and differences between the two.
• Read your favorite poem/story to the class and explain why you like it.	• Critically evaluate two local restaurants (or two sports teams, etc.) and present your findings.
• Choose your favorite subject at school and decide on a topic to teach to your classmates (e.g., the ecosystem, the First World War, the World Cup, how to play a violin).	• Choose a term in your field of study and define it. Provide examples and visual support. Take questions from your audience.

Reinhardt (2013), "organizing a speech is probably the single most important task of a good presenter" (p. 3), so time definitely needs to be allotted to organizing the talk. Research has also shown that difference in the level of syntactic and morphological errors is not as important as clear discourse moves for greater listener comprehension (Williams, 1992). That is, a well-organized discourse structure makes it easier for listeners to process discourse information through stress placement and intonation (Cutler et al., 1997). Hence, during the practice phase, it would be beneficial for students to decide on organizational cues as well as on appropriate stress for phrases and difficult words, and correct intonation patterns for their lists, contradictory statements, requests, and so on. That way, their chances at improved intelligibility will be greater. (For a comprehensive coverage of phrase and word stress rules, see Hahn & Dickerson, 1999.)

Also, as intonation is best taught in discourse (Levis & Pickering, 2004), it is recommended that teachers scaffold intonation assignment early in the project and once a draft of the script has been developed. For example, the teacher could explicitly teach students how to predict and pronounce prosodic features, such as stress and intonation, in words and phrases through strategy guidelines and modeling. The goal is for learners to later follow the guidelines during their practice time in private (Sardegna, 2012). Additionally, as reported by Sardegna and McGregor (2013), effective strategy training and use can help students become aware of their pronunciation challenges and thus become more efficient in correcting them.

Finally, during private practice students can engage in self-teaching by applying rules and strategies, by reading the words and phrases aloud repeatedly and systematically, and by self-monitoring and self-correcting until their speech becomes fluent and closer to the models provided by the teacher. If possible, students could also video-record their presentations during practice and both self-assess and peer-assess their work with the help of a rubric. Analyzing and reflecting on their own and on others' video-recorded presentations have been shown to increase learner awareness of errors and promote focused practice to remedy the errors (Sardegna & McGregor, 2013). Ideally, students should also video-record their final oral presentation so that they can later assess their live performance and reflect on their strengths and weaknesses. It is highly recommended that these assessments be scaffolded by the teacher with a rubric or focused questions such as "Do you hear a lot of repetitions and/or pauses?" and "Can you hear a clear emphasis in the phrase?" Assessments that are enhanced through teacher guides or rubrics help learners not only notice more readily their own errors, but also provide more consistent and specific feedback to their peers.

This section highlighted the connections between the components of a successful oral presentation and the components of intelligible speech, and it discussed how their interconnectedness makes oral presentation skills and pronunciation skills indissociable and, thus, excellent candidates for integration. To improve in one skill area, one should target the other skill area concomitantly. The next section focuses on prominence and discusses why and how it can be taught, practiced, and improved while preparing for an oral presentation.

Targeting Prominence in Oral Presentations

Prosodic features (i.e., the patterns of stress and intonation) are integral elements in the organization of English academic discourse (Levis & Pickering, 2004) and have been found to have a direct impact on comprehensibility (Wennerstrom, 1998). (See Chapter 3 for more information.) They signal topic shift, old versus given information, contrasts, and continuity in speech (see Chapters 5 and 6). These signals ease listener comprehension because they cue information structure and provide speech cohesion (Williams, 1992). Of all the prosodic features, prominence—also generally referred to as primary phrase stress (PS)—is considered the most essential for oral communication because of its role in calling attention to new information, which promotes listener comprehension (Hahn, 2004). Studies have shown that when students become aware of this speech feature and learn how, when, and why a word becomes prominent, their PS placement improves in a short time (Sardegna, 2012; Sardegna & McGregor, 2013) and is maintained over time (Sardegna, 2012). Comprehensibility ratings studies have also shown that the wider the pitch range, the less accented native speakers perceive the speaker to be (Kang, 2010). Therefore, it is crucial that teachers teach this prosodic feature.

A PS is marked by higher pitch, vowel lengthening, and greater amplitude (Kang, 2010). Unless there is a reason not to highlight new information, PS falls on the last content word (LC; i.e., a noun, adjective, verb, or adverb), or last function word (LF; i.e., other words such as an article, preposition, conjunction, etc.) if there is no content word, in the string of new information (Hahn & Dickerson, 1999). To illustrate, consider the first slide of an oral presentation featuring the American alligator (Figure 1). The suggested oral introduction for this slide contains 11 phrases or thought groups. In this figure (and the ones following), the PS is bolded, and the end of a thought group is marked with a period or with the symbol |. In English, new information is usually found at the end of the phrase (Hahn & Dickerson, 1999), as in phrases 1 and 2. Note that the LC words in these two phrases are *animal* and *alligator*. Consequently, these words receive focus (PS) to draw attention to the new information that they are conveying. However, as the word *alligator* is already known in the discourse by phrase 4, the focus in phrases 4 and 6 does not fall on *alligator*.

Figure 1 Oral Presentation Slide Introducing the American Alligator

The American Alligator

Joe Student
Grade 6

1. Do you know what **animal** this is?	1. animal (LC)
2. It's an **alligator**.	2. alligator (LC)
3. **Today**, ❘ ↘↗	3. Today (LC)
4. I will give a presentation on the **American** alligator.	4. American (LC)
5. **First**, ❘ ↘↗	5. First (LC)
6. I will give you some **facts** about the American alligator.	6. facts (LC)
7. **Second**, ❘ ↘↗	7. Second (LC)
8. I will show you the **size** of the American alligator.	8. size (LC)
9. **Finally**, ↘↗	9. Finally (LC)
10. I will compare the American **alligator** ❘	10. alligator (EC)
11. to the American **crocodile**.	11. crocodile (EC)

Instead, it falls on *American* and *facts,* respectively. The words (or syllables) that follow a PS are always destressed, which is a marker of old information.

Also note that the discourse organization in Figure 1 is marked with discourse cues (e.g., *today, first, second, finally*). Discourse markings of this kind, which are used to indicate continuity of speech and identify progression and relationships among different phrases, have been shown to be an important element of comprehensibility because they ease interpretation (Terken & Hirschberg, 1994). These discourse cues are generally taught in oral communication classes because they are easily learnable and help overcome misplaced or absent prosodic cues. In other words, in the absence of a distinct PS, these discourse cues help mark more explicit pauses and links between ideas. We contend that when these discourse markings (e.g., *first, second, third*) are taught, they should be taught with their distinct prosody (i.e., with a fall-rise intonation ↘↗), thereby integrating oral communication skills with pronunciation skills (see 3, 5, 7, and 9 in Figure 1). Additionally, as shown in Figure 2, each component (formed by one or more words) on a list constitutes a thought group, and the PS falls on the last content word (LC) in each thought group (e.g., *fish, turtles, snakes, mammals*). A rise-to-mid intonation (↗), as in 2, 3, and 4, is used for each member of the list, except for the last member (5) which receives a falling intonation (↘).

PS is also used to draw the listener's attention to explicit contrasts (EC; see addi-

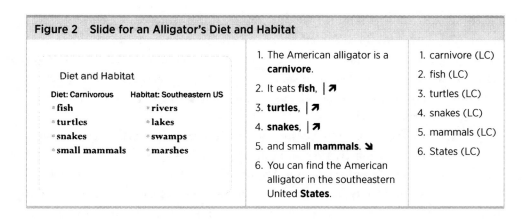

Figure 2   Slide for an Alligator's Diet and Habitat

Diet and Habitat Diet: Carnivorous Habitat: Southeastern US * fish * rivers * turtles * lakes * snakes * swamps * small mammals * marshes	1. The American alligator is a **carnivore**. 2. It eats **fish**, | ↗ 3. **turtles**, | ↗ 4. **snakes**, | ↗ 5. and small **mammals**. ↘ 6. You can find the American alligator in the southeastern United **States**.	1. carnivore (LC) 2. fish (LC) 3. turtles (LC) 4. snakes (LC) 5. mammals (LC) 6. States (LC)

tional examples in Chapters 3, 5, and 6). If the contrasting element is more than one word, the primary stress and pitch move go on the LC (or on the last function word if there is no LC). Only the contrasted item carries the PS, whether it is a word or part of a word, and regardless of whether it conveys old or new information (Hahn & Dickerson, 1999). Contrasting elements can be found in choice questions, either/or statements, [x, not y] or [not x, but y] statements, contradictions, parallel phrases,

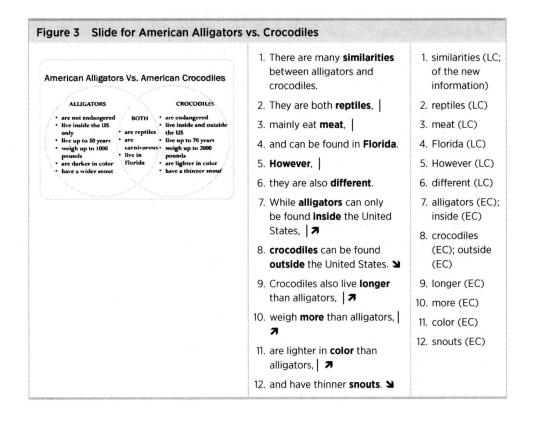

Figure 3   Slide for American Alligators vs. Crocodiles

American Alligators Vs. American Crocodiles **ALLIGATORS** **BOTH** **CROCODILES** • are not endangered • live inside the US only • live up to 50 years • weigh up to 1000 pounds • are darker in color • have a wider snout • are reptiles • are carnivorous • live in Florida • are endangered • live inside and outside the US • live up to 70 years • weigh up to 2000 pounds • are lighter in color • have a thinner snout	1. There are many **similarities** between alligators and crocodiles. 2. They are both **reptiles**, | 3. mainly eat **meat**, | 4. and can be found in **Florida**. 5. **However**, | 6. they are also **different**. 7. While **alligators** can only be found **inside** the United States, | ↗ 8. **crocodiles** can be found **outside** the United States. ↘ 9. Crocodiles also live **longer** than alligators, | ↗ 10. weigh **more** than alligators, | ↗ 11. are lighter in **color** than alligators, | ↗ 12. and have thinner **snouts**. ↘	1. similarities (LC; of the new information) 2. reptiles (LC) 3. meat (LC) 4. Florida (LC) 5. However (LC) 6. different (LC) 7. alligators (EC); inside (EC) 8. crocodiles (EC); outside (EC) 9. longer (EC) 10. more (EC) 11. color (EC) 12. snouts (EC)

and comparative nouns. If more than one contrast is in a sentence, a rise-to-mid intonation (➚) is used for the first element and a falling intonation (➘) for the second (see 7–8 and 9–12 in Figure 3). When two nouns are compared, if the nouns are old (as in 9–12 in Figure 3), the adjective carries the PS (Levis & Pickering, 2004). Sometimes there are two contrasts in a single thought group (as in 7–8, in Figure 3; Hahn & Dickerson, 1999).

Finally, it has been posited that destressing also occurs before a PS when a strongly stressed syllable immediately preceding the PS is destressed so that the PS can be heard more clearly. This phenomenon has been termed *upstream destressing*, and it "happens most commonly to the content word or loud function word nearest the primary stress on the left" (Dickerson, 2011, p. 73). For example, in "It's a coat for my cousin Susan," *Susan* is in focus and the content word preceding it (*cousin*) is destressed. More empirical data validating this claim is needed.

Figure 4   Guidelines for Practice

1. Teach and model strategies before students have to use them for practice.
2. Ask students to predict and underline/circle PS words and draw lines separating thought groups (see suggested practice slides at the end of the chapter for predicting PS).
3. Ask students to read the phrases aloud.
4. Assign comparison slides (e.g., with graphs, Venn diagrams, figures, columns, tables).
5. Provide speech models available online or recorded by you for students to use as guides.
6. Assign read-alouds with and without marked PS words for controlled practice.

Figure 5   Guidelines for Preparing Oral Presentations

Ask students to . . .

1. Prepare a script and identify thought groups and key words in the script.
2. Predict which words should be PS words and which words should be destressed. (Note: If you taught other pronunciation features, such as linking, word stress, and intonation, tell students to predict these features as well.)
3. Practice the script many times aloud until fluent.
4. (Video-) Record a practice presentation. View/listen to it and critique it. Then re-record it as many times as needed until fluent.
5. Reflect on weaknesses and strengths as well as on effective strategies to improve weaknesses.
6. Seek feedback from teacher and peers.

Figure 6   Guidelines for After Giving an Oral Presentation

Ask students to . . .

1. View/listen to their live presentation and evaluate it, preferably with a rubric.

2. Reflect on the feedback received.

3. Write a reflection on the process and the outcome.

4. Consider areas in need of improvement and future work.

Pedagogical Suggestions

To conclude, Figures 4–6 provide pedagogical guidelines for integrating pronunciation practice in oral presentation tasks.

Finally, for further practice, students can use the slides below (answer key follows).

Practice Slides

Mark the primary phrase stress in each thought group, and indicate the rule you followed (LC or EC).

A Tale of Two Countries

Joe Student
Jane Student

1. Today, we will give a presentation |
2. about South Korea and Turkey.
3. First, |
4. we will present some general information about our countries.
5. Second, |
6. we will discuss some data related to our countries.
7. Finally, |
8. we will compare and contrast our two home countries.

Joe's Country: South Korea

- Popular Festivals:
  - Boseong Green Tea Festival
  - Pohang International Fireworks Festival
  - Gwangju World Kimchi Culture Festival
  - Jinju Lantern Festival

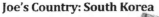

9. Many festivals take place in South Korea every year.
10. Some popular festivals include the Boseong Green Tea Festival, |
11. the Pohang International Fireworks Festival, |
12. the Gwangju World Kimchi Culture Festival, |
13. and the Jinju Lantern Festival.

continued

Jane's Country: Turkey

- Popular Attractions:
  - Fethiye
  - Nemrut
  - Lake Eğirdir
  - Kartalkaya

14. There are many beautiful places in Turkey.

15. Some popular attractions include Fethiye, |

16. Nemrut, |

17. Lake Eğirdir, |

18. and Kartalkaya.

South Korea and Turkey: Facts

Category	South Korea	Turkey
Population	49,039,986	81,619,392
Land Area	99,720 sq km	783,562 sq km
Language(s)	Korean	Turkish, Kurdish, etc.
Mother's Mean Age at 1st birth	29.6	22.9
Internet Users	39.4 million	27.233 million

19. We will now discuss some interesting facts about South Korea and Turkey.

20. Turkey has more people than South Korea.

21. Turkey has approximately 81 million people, |

22. while South Korea has approximately 49 million people.

23. Turkey is also bigger than South Korea.

24. Turkey is approximately 780,000 square kilometers, |

25. while South Korea is approximately 100,000 square kilometers.

26. In South Korea, |

27. people speak Korean, |

28. but in Turkey, |

29. there are people who speak Turkish, |

30. people who speak Kurdish, |

31. and people who speak other languages.

32. Mothers also have babies at a younger age in Turkey.

33. On average, |

34. Turkish women have their first baby when they are around 22, |

35. but Korean women have their first baby when they are around 29.

36. There are also more Korean Internet users than Turkish Internet users.

37. There are 39.4 million Internet users in South Korea, |

38. while there are 27.2 million Internet users in Turkey.

continued

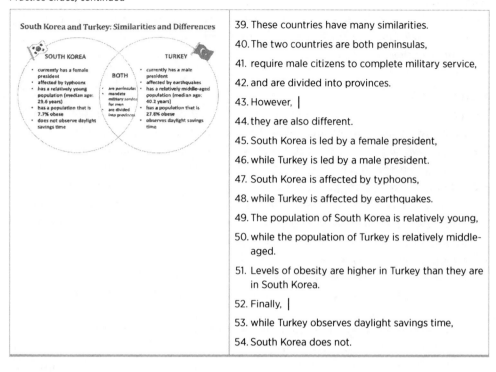

39. These countries have many similarities.

40. The two countries are both peninsulas,

41. require male citizens to complete military service,

42. and are divided into provinces.

43. However, |

44. they are also different.

45. South Korea is led by a female president,

46. while Turkey is led by a male president.

47. South Korea is affected by typhoons,

48. while Turkey is affected by earthquakes.

49. The population of South Korea is relatively young,

50. while the population of Turkey is relatively middle-aged.

51. Levels of obesity are higher in Turkey than they are in South Korea.

52. Finally, |

53. while Turkey observes daylight savings time,

54. South Korea does not.

ANSWER KEY

1. presentation (LC); 2. Turkey (LC); 3. First (LC); 4. information (LC); 5. Second (LC); 6. data (LC); 7. Finally (LC); 8. contrast (LC); 9. year (LC); 10. Tea (LC); 11. Fireworks (LC); 12. Culture (LC); 13. Lantern (LC); 14. Turkey (LC); 15. Fethiye (LC); 16. Nemrut (LC); 17. Eğirdir (LC); 18. Kartalkaya (LC); 19. interesting (LC); 20. people (EC); 21. Turkey, 81 (EC); 22. Korea, 49 (EC); 23. bigger (EC); 24. Turkey, 780,000 (EC); 25. Korea, 100,000 (EC); 26. Korea (EC); 27. Korean (EC); 28. Turkey (EC); 29. Turkish (EC); 30. Kurdish (EC); 31. other (EC); 32. age (LC); 33. average (LC); 34. Turkish, 22 (EC); 35. Korean, 29 (EC); 36. Korean, Turkish (EC); 37. 39.4, Korea (EC); 38. 27.2, Turkey (EC); 39. similarities (LC); 40. peninsulas (LC); 41. military (LC); 42. provinces (LC); 43. However (LC); 44. different (LC); 45. Korea, female (EC); 46. Turkey, male (EC); 47. Korea, typhoons (EC); 48. Turkey, earthquakes (EC); 49. Korea, young (EC); 50. Turkey, middle-aged (EC); 51. higher, Turkey, Korea (EC); 52. Finally (LC); 53. Turkey, savings (EC); 54. Korea, not (EC)

Conclusion

This chapter proposed a model for integrating presentation skills with pronunciation skills that is based on the premise that learners need to take charge of their learning and become independent self-teachers. However, for their autonomous practice to be focused and targeted (and therefore effective), teachers should provide explicit knowledge of linguistic features and strategies, offer models and guidelines for practice, and create opportunities for learners to practice and evaluate their oral presentation and pronunciation skills concomitantly.

Resource

Celce-Murcia, M., Brinton, D. M., & Goodwin, J. M. (2010). *Teaching pronunciation: A course book and reference guide* (2nd ed.). Cambridge, England: Cambridge University Press.

References

Cutler, A., Oahan, D., & van Donselaar, W. (1997). Prosody in the comprehension of spoken language: A literature review. *Language and Speech, 40,* 141–201.

Derwing, T. M., & Munro, M. J. (2005). Second language accent and pronunciation teaching: A research-based approach. *TESOL Quarterly, 39,* 379–397.

Derwing, T. M., & Munro, M. J. (2014). Myth 1: Once you have been speaking a second language for years, it's too late to change your pronunciation. In L. Grant (Ed.), *Pronunciation myths: Applying second language research to classroom teaching* (pp. 34–55). Ann Arbor: University of Michigan Press.

Dickerson, W. B. (2011). Upstream destressing: Another step toward natural speech. In. J. Levis & K. LeVelle (Eds.), *Proceedings of the 2nd Pronunciation in Second Language Learning and Teaching Conference* (pp. 70–81), Ames: Iowa State University.

Hahn, L. (2004). Primary stress and intelligibility: Research to motivate the teaching of suprasegmentals. *TESOL Quarterly, 38,* 201–223.

Hahn, L., & Dickerson, W. (1999). *Speechcraft: Discourse pronunciation for advanced learners.* Ann Arbor: University of Michigan Press.

Jiménez Raya, M. (2011). Enhancing pedagogy for autonomy: The potential of a case-based approach in promoting reflection and action. *Innovation in Language Learning and Teaching, 5,* 151–163.

Kang, O. (2010). Relative salience of suprasegmental features on judgments of L2 comprehensibility and accentedness. *System, 38,* 301–315.

Levis, J. M. (2005). Changing contexts and shifting paradigms in pronunciation teaching. *TESOL Quarterly, 39,* 369–378.

Levis, J. M., & Grant, L. (2003). Integrating pronunciation into ESL/EFL classrooms. *TESOL Journal, 12,* 13–19.

Levis, J., & Pickering, L. (2004). Teaching intonation in discourse using speech visualization technology. *System, 32,* 505–524.

Munro, M. J., & Derwing, T. M. (2006). The functional load principle in ESL pronunciation instruction: An exploratory study. *System, 34,* 520–531.

Murphy, J. (1991). Oral communication in TESOL: Integrating speaking, listening and pronunciation. *TESOL Quarterly, 25,* 51–75.

Murphy, J. (2014). Myth 7: Teacher training programs provide adequate preparation. In L. Grant (Ed.), *Pronunciation myths: Applying second language research to classroom teaching* (pp. 188–217). Ann Arbor: University of Michigan Press.

Reinhardt, S. M. (2013). *Giving academic presentations* (2nd ed.). Ann Arbor: Michigan University Press.

Sardegna, V. G. (2011). Pronunciation learning strategies that improve ESL learners' linking. In J. Levis & K. LeVelle (Eds.), *Proceedings of the 2nd Pronunciation in Second Language Learning and Teaching Conference* (pp. 105–121). Ames: Iowa State University.

Sardegna, V. G. (2012). Learner differences in strategy use, self-efficacy beliefs, and pronunciation improvement. In J. Levis & K. LeVelle (Eds.), *Proceedings of the 3rd Pronunciation in Second Language Learning and Teaching Conference* (pp. 39–53). Ames: Iowa State University.

Sardegna, V. G., & McGregor, A. (2013). Scaffolding students' self-regulated efforts for effective pronunciation practice. In J. Levis & K. LeVelle (Eds.), *Proceedings of the 4th Pronunciation in Second Language Learning and Teaching Conference* (pp. 182–193). Ames: Iowa State University.

Terken, J. M. B., & Hirschberg, J. (1994). Deaccentuation of words representing "given" information: Effects of persistence of grammatical function and surface position. *Language and Speech, 37*, 125–145.

Watts, P., & Huensch, A. (2013). Integrated speaking, listening and pronunciation: Are textbooks leading the way? In J. Levis & K. LeVelle (Eds.), *Proceedings of the 4th Pronunciation in Second Language Learning and Teaching Conference* (pp. 265–278). Ames: Iowa State University.

Wennerstrom, A. (1998). Intonation as cohesion in academic discourse: A study of Chinese speakers of English. *Studies in Second Language Acquisition, 42*, 1–13.

Williams, J. (1992). Planning, discourse marking, and the comprehensibility of international teaching assistants. *TESOL Quarterly, 26*, 693–711.

Zielinski, B. (2008). The listener: No longer the silent partner in reduced intelligibility. *System, 36*, 69–84.

CHAPTER 5

Pronunciation, Thought Grouping, and General Listening Skills

John Murphy

This chapter focuses on connections between listening, pronunciation, and how to coordinate their instruction in the teaching of English as a second language (ESL). The next chapter, Chapter 6, highlights attention to pronunciation and listening for content. In contrast, the present chapter foregrounds attention not to products of listening comprehension but to the listening process itself (see Field, 2008) by focusing on acoustic qualities of spoken English for purposes of more effective instruction in listening and pronunciation. It explores the nature of their acoustic signal, how their acoustic properties overlap, and how to apply such understandings more efficiently in ESL classrooms.

The Process of Thought Grouping

Although there are many connections between listening and pronunciation, a medium they share is the process of thought grouping. A conventional view is that sounds and words constitute the medium through which we exchange messages with others, but the process of thought grouping plays just as critical a role (Murphy, 2013). Because it operates beneath the level of conscious awareness, most people (English language teachers included) are unaware of the thought grouping process and of its pervasive impacts on communication. One of its essential features is that we speak in rhythmic pulses of speech. Some of our speech pulses contain a small number of words (e.g., *Look out!*) while others contain a larger number (e.g., *If you would be so kind as to proceed with caution*). Regardless of their length, each of these rhythmic pulses of speech is straddled by brief pauses. A related feature of the rhythm of English speech is that pauses between thought groups may manifest in several different ways. One way is a momentary break in the stream of speech, sometimes accompanied by an intake of breath. Another is to lengthen, or hold, the final syllable of one thought group before the next begins. As Lane (2010) explains, all of these moments of transition between thought groups may be perceived by the listener as a pause even if the speaker's voice is actually doing something more along the lines of "linger[ing] on" or lengthening a transitional syllable, rather than completely interrupting the flow of breath (p. 52). From this point forward, I refer to these characteristic pulses of speech as *thought groups* and to the breaches or juncture breaks between them as *pauses*.[1] Consciously or unconsciously, deliberately or beneath the level of our awareness, the process of thought grouping is foundational to everything we listen to and say in English.

Math Equations to Illustrate the Process of Thought Grouping

Wong (1987) and Gilbert (2008) provide a handy way to introduce the process of thought grouping to ESL students: referencing simple math equations (Table 1).

Once learners recognize that different patterns of thought grouping may lead to genuine differences in meaning, they can practice (and also generate) additional examples on their own (Table 2).

Another strategy is to use well-known folk sayings and proverbs (see Figure 1). Through focused discussion in pairs or small groups, students can figure out probable pause locations between thought groups on their own. For discussion of a comparable set of classroom activities, see Chapter 7.

Table 1   Two Illustrations of Math Equations

WHAT IT LOOKS LIKE	WHAT IT SOUNDS LIKE
$(2 + 3) \times 4 = 20$	"Two plus three // times four // equals twenty."
$2 + (3 \times 4) = 14$	"Two plus // three times four // equals fourteen."

Note. Double slash marks (//) signal a pause between thought groups.

Table 2   Math Equations to Illustrate Thought Grouping

WHAT IT LOOKS LIKE	WHAT IT SOUNDS LIKE
$(2 + 4) \times 5 = 30$	
$2 + (4 \times 5) = 22$	
$(3 + 8) \times 2 = 22$	
$3 + (8 \times 2) = 19$	

---

1   Some alternative ways of labeling what is referred to here as *thought groups* include *speech units, tone groups, tone units, intonation units,* and *language chunks.*

The Internet provides dozens of sites dedicated to such folk sayings and proverbs. Here are a few proverbs in which the number in parentheses signals a probable number of thought groups.

- An apple a day keeps the doctor away. (2)
- When the going gets tough the tough get going. (2 or possibly 3)
- Early to bed and early to rise makes a man healthy wealthy and wise. (5)
- Ask not what your country can do for you ask what you can do for your country. (4)

Eventually, learners need to recognize that participants in English conversations both produce and interpret the spoken language through a process of thought grouping. In this sense, it is a process that lies at the intersection of listening and pronunciation. Once the thought grouping process is introduced, learners find it easier to understand related speech phenomena such as word stress, prominence, reductions, rhythm, linking, and intonation (Dickerson, 2010).

Length of Speaking Turns

Conversation is probably the most familiar context of interpersonal communication, listening, and pronunciation. A conversational feature everyone shares is that we participate in the sometimes messy process of taking turns while speaking and listening to others. A characteristic that distinguishes more proficient ESL speakers from their less proficient peers is the relative length of their respective speaking turns. More proficient speakers are better able to take longer turns and are more adept at listening attentively to know how and when to initiate, borrow, offer, overlap, relinquish, hold on to, step on someone else's, dismiss, or even "steal" a speaking turn during conversation. As second language (L2) proficiency increases and as learners gain confidence in how to participate in conversations, their capacity for taking longer speaking turns increases. Along with the challenge of taking longer speaking turns, students need to become more aware as listeners to act more strategically as turn takers.

Speaking turns and the process of thought grouping are related phenomena with implications for teaching listening and pronunciation. A turn taken while speaking necessarily comprises at least one thought group, though a single turn might include a few or even a very large number of thought groups strung together. If a person is telling a story, for example, the number of thought groups in a speaking turn may be quite large. But even as thought groups string together, any individual thought group continues to contain a relatively small number of words. A thought group made of more than 10–15 words, for example, would be rather long.[2] Regardless of the raw number of words they contain, most thought groups contain two or fewer perceptible beats. The rhythmic beats of English speech fall on the primary stressed syllables of prominent words. Effective communication demands that listeners recognize the cues provided by such beats and that they also be able to discern the less distinct (or blurred) spans of phonological information residing between them. The following are some of the most frequent six-word thought groups of spoken English (O'Keeffe, McCarthy, & Carter, 2007), with their rhythmic beats (i.e., primary stressed syllables of prominent words) signaled through bold print.

// do you **know** what I **mean** //
// at the **end** of the **day** //
// **I** don't know what it **is** // or // I **don't** know what it **is** //
// in the **mid**dle of the **night** //[3]
// on the **oth**er side of the //

Cauldwell (2002) estimates are that over 80% of the thought groups of spontaneous speech contain just two or fewer prominent words (i.e., two or fewer perceptible beats). Those containing three prominent words "are relatively rare, and account for fewer than 10%" of thought groups of spoken English, while those with as many as four prominent words "account for about 1%" (Cauldwell, 2013, pp. 40, 41). Thought groups made up of five or more prominent words are even rarer. To maintain the floor during a conversation, ESL speakers need to learn to (a) speak in thought groups, (b) link consecutive thought groups together, (c) recognize the more salient bits of information carried by an interlocutor's rhythmic beats, (d) discern the blurred spans of language appearing between such beats, and (e) pronounce their own thought groups with an intelligible rhythm. To be effective, listening instruction needs to feature practice in discerning information carried not only by speakers'

---

2   Cauldwell (2013) identifies an upper limit for thought group length at about 20 syllables.
3   Since *middle* is a two-syllable word, only its initial stressed syllable carries prominence. The same happens with the word *other* immediately below.

more salient acoustic beats but also by the blurrier, and therefore more challenging, acoustic stretches of the language signal between them. The former is a traditional focus of ESL listening (i.e., comprehension) instruction, while the latter focuses on the listening process and is rarely taught (Field, 2008).

Instructional Resources

The first step of the instructional sequence I follow for building learner awareness of the process of thought grouping is to locate a series of language samples relevant to learners' proficiency level(s), interests, and needs. Part of a teacher's role is to search widely and to become a bit of an archivist who locates, collects, and stores such resources. Possibilities for locating appropriate language samples (both spoken and written) are nearly limitless given the ease of contemporary Internet access and the multimedia nature of growing numbers of ESL resource materials. When gathering and arranging to work with such materials, care needs to be taken to protect the legitimate intellectual property rights of publishers and authors.[4]

There are advantages in working with language samples for which paired sets of audio and transcribed electronic versions are readily available (e.g., online U.S. Presidential Inaugural and State of the Union addresses, TED talks, corpus resources, National Public Radio broadcasts, commencement addresses).[5] At lower proficiency levels, even introductory dialogues and reading passages may be used with the procedures I am about to describe.

Creating "Punctuation-Free" Language Samples

Once a suitable audio recording supported by a written (preferably electronic) transcript has been located, the next step is crucial. To be able to introduce and teach connections between thought grouping, listening, and pronunciation, I modify the original transcript to render it nearly punctuation free. When preparing the transcript of a TED talk, for example, it takes just a few moments to copy the talk's e-transcript and paste it into a word-processing document. Once saved as an electronic file, I double-space it and insert line numbers in the page margin. But the most important step is to remove all of the document's periods, commas, semicolons, colons, quotation marks, capital letters, extra spaces between sentences, and paragraph breaks (i.e., nearly all forms of printed punctuation). While the removal of most punctuation is essential, it is useful to leave in apostrophes that signal possessives and contracted forms. What remains are all of the transcript's original words, but the revised version contains almost no punctuation at all.

---

4 For a reliable discussion of copyright and fair use guidelines, go to www.teachingcopyright.org.
5 For commencement speeches, go to www.graduationwisdom.com/speeches/topten.htm.

These materials are the punctuation-free language samples designed for classroom use. Once a sufficient number of copies are ready, I select a format for presenting the audio sample in class (e.g., live delivery, YouTube broadcast, audio player, PC or laptop). (For a grammar-focused twist on such procedures, see Chapters 9 and 12.) Figures 2 and 3 are two examples of punctuation-free transcripts.

Application Task 1: Identifying and Learning to Work With Thought Groups

Instruction begins with a listening discrimination activity. Soon after the teacher distributes a punctuation-free transcript, students notice that something is different. Their questions provide opportunities to discuss the following:

- why punctuation has been removed

- what thought groups are

- how the process of thought grouping impacts spoken English

Figure 2   Challenges of Learning Science: Punctuation-Free Transcript Segment of an Online Video Lecture

<u>man I hate science yeah me too science is so stupid it doesn't make any sense I know I'll never be good at science</u> have you ever been part of a conversation like this lots of people have learning and studying scientific concepts requires a special type of thinking that doesn't come easily to everyone you may be surprised to know that even people who study science for a living often struggle with the complicated formulas and theories most people find science class fun when they are little but in high school and college scientific study gets way more difficult

Note. The underlined section is a dialogue between two people, the remainder is a monologue.
Source: Koch (n.d.).

Figure 3   Earthquake! Punctuation-Free Transcript of a Dialogue for Low-Intermediate ESL

hey do you feel that I can't believe it yeah the ground is shaking we're having an earthquake what should we do don't panic let's stand in the doorway my mother says a doorway is the safest place but I still feel it this is a strong earthquake is it ever going to stop oh wait a minute I think it stopped now yeah it stopped glad that's over were you scared just a little earthquakes are scary

Source: Adapted from *ESL Dialogue: Earthquake!* (2012).

- why thought grouping is the activity's focus

- how the activity relates to L2 listening and L2 pronunciation

I use the first few lines of the sample text to provide a few illustrations of thought groups. Once the class is ready, I ask students to listen to the full audio recording (alternatively, a spoken version can be presented live in the classroom). Their purpose the first time through is to listen for global comprehension and to be able to summarize/discuss the selection's gist. Once they are comfortable with its content, students listen again for the purpose of delineating thought groups. Their task is to listen carefully and use pencils to insert slanted lines (//) at the end of each thought group they notice the speaker use. Students may need to listen to the recording either in sections or several different times to complete this task successfully. If they find the task too difficult, then the language sample is likely beyond their level of proficiency and a more suitable one (e.g., less linguistically complex; on a more familiar topic) should be substituted. One of the features we identify and discuss during these early stages is that pauses between thought groups can be of varying lengths.

Figure 4 offers a portion of the science lecture depicted in Figure 2 with pauses between thought groups indicated.

Similarly, Figure 5 presents a portion of the dialogue from Figure 3 with pauses between thought groups indicated.

Figure 4   Challenges of Learning Science:
Thought Groups Indicated With Double Slash Marks

// man // I hate science // yeah // me too // science is so stupid // it doesn't make any sense // I know // I'll never be good at science // have you ever been part of a conversation like this // lots of people have // learning and studying scientific concepts // requires a special type of thinking that doesn't come easily to everyone // you may be surprised to know that even people who study science for a living //

Figure 5   Earthquake! Thought Groups
Indicated With Double Slash Marks

// hey do you feel that // I can't believe it // yeah // the ground is shaking // we're having an earthquake // what should we do // don't panic // let's stand in the doorway // my mother says a doorway is the safest place // but I still feel it // this is a strong earthquake //

Such procedures may be used as recurring in-class activities, one-on-one tutoring, and/or private study at home. Here are some topics that are useful to discuss with the class during the activity:

- We do not speak in continuous, uninterrupted streams of speech.
- Thought groups (TGs) are the building blocks of both listening and pronunciation.
- TGs constitute the primary phonological context of English pronunciation.
- A TG is a cluster of words grouped together within a pulse of speech.
- Pauses straddle TGs.
- What listeners perceive as a pause does not necessarily coincide with a complete stoppage in the flow of speech.
- Since a speaker is the agent of thought grouping, the process is flexible.
- With practice, ESL listeners are able to improve their abilities to perceive TGs.
- TGs link consecutively to form a speaking turn.
- Analysis of audio recordings engenders better understanding of the process.
- More effective speakers use patterns of thought grouping to more fully engage listeners.
- A TG can be as short as a single word or syllable (e.g., // man // I hate science // yeah // me too //).
- Speakers in more formal settings, or who are addressing large audiences, tend to use shorter TGs (they pause more frequently).
- TGs that are excessively long can be more difficult to follow.
- Listeners may also have difficulties when there are too many TGs (i.e., too many pauses).
- The length of a TG is normally fewer than 12–15 words (fewer than 20 syllables).
- With increased awareness, ESL learners
  — *as speakers,* learn to be more strategic in using TGs;
  — *as listeners,* are better able to accurately perceive and interpret the thought grouping cues speakers provide;
  — *as pronouncers of English,* are better able to understand and apply what they have studied about English pronunciation in phonological contexts of the thought group.

Along with the teaching procedures described so far, some other options include the following:

- Pairs or teams of students can compare their individual efforts to discuss points of agreement and disagreement.

- Students can work at individual computer stations, a procedure that permits easy access to the original recording, repeated listening, and even closer analysis.

- Once Application Task 1's listening discrimination procedures becomes routine
  — teachers can introduce language samples that differ along such dimensions as source, speech register, genre, situational context, and complexity;
  — students can locate their own audio-plus-transcript materials and share them with other members of the class.

Eventually, once students have grown familiar with any single recording, they can begin to use their marked-up copies of its transcript for pronunciation practice. Though their initial focus is the process of thought grouping, their efforts can later shift to other facets of pronunciation learning (e.g., prominence, phonemic linking across word boundaries, other naturally occurring phonological processes).

Application Task 2: Speaker Agency in the Process of Thought Grouping

In the list of principles presented above, one item highlighted the flexible nature of the process of thought grouping and the role of speaker agency. Application Task 2 is grounded in these principles. Over 40 years of research into the phonology of English signals that all such phenomena are "speaker-controlled, purpose-driven, interactive, co-operative, context-related, and context-changing" (Cauldwell, 2000, p. 1).

To foreground the active role speakers ultimately take on as agents of thought grouping, rhythm, and prominence, Application Task 2 presents opportunities for learners to exercise such agency. While continuing to work with transcripts they previously marked up in Application Task 1, students begin to identify alternative ways of forming thought groups. By doing so they have opportunities to explore some of the possibilities and constraints in the thought grouping process. To help set the stage for this task, Figure 6 demonstrates that the original Challenges in Learning Science lecture (Figure 2) contained several thought groups that were rather long.

Students revisit the transcript for the purpose of identifying alternative ways that thought groups might have been delineated by a different speaker or under alternative circumstances. Figure 7 reveals how one group of ESL learners re-envisioned the larger set of thought groups originally depicted in Figure 4.

Figure 6   Three Illustrations of Longer Thought Groups

. . . // requires a special type of thinking that doesn't come easily to everyone // you may be surprised to know that even people who study science for a living // . . . . most people find science class fun when they are little // . . .

Figure 7   One Group of ESL Learners' Way of Delineating Thought Groups

// man // I hate science // yeah // me too // science is so stupid // it doesn't make any sense // I know // I'll never be good at science // *have you // ever been part of a conversation like this* // *lots of people have* // learning and studying scientific concepts // *requires a special type of thinking // that doesn't come easily to everyone* // *you may be surprised to know // that even people who study science for a living* // . . .

Note. Differences from Figure 4 are underlined and italicized.

As Figure 7 reveals, the students' strategy was to insert more pauses. Such activities can foster learner agency as they transition away from more controlled listening discrimination phases. Application Task 2 also illustrates that there are constraints and patterns in how thought groups may be formed. Through guided analysis and discussion, students begin to realize that pauses cannot be inserted haphazardly. Words that English speakers cluster together to form thought groups tend to coalesce as noun phrases, verb phrases, relative clauses, simple (e.g., short) sentences, lexical bundles, prepositional phrases, and so on. Ultimately, however, it is less a matter of syntactic categories that guides the process and more a reflection of the communicative impact speakers are trying to have on listeners.

Application to Additional Listening and Pronunciation Phenomena

Once students are familiar with the process of thought grouping, the nature of instruction can deepen by featuring connections with other related phenomena. A priority is prominence. As discussed by other contributors to this volume (e.g., Chapters 3, 4, and 6), prominent words are pronounced with increased volume and clarity relative to other words within the same thought group. In combination with the process of thought grouping, these qualities result in the distinctive rhythm of

English. Following conventions for the presentation and analysis of thought groups proposed by Cauldwell (2013), Figure 8 depicts a single thought group; its columns are numbered from right to left, and the focus syllable of the thought group's prominent word appears in the shaded section in column 2.

In Figure 8, the word *doorway* is the prominent word. However, as column 2 indicates, it is only the word's primary stressed syllable *door* that serves as the carrier of prominence. The same word's unstressed syllable *way* is non-prominent and therefore is shifted to the column to the right. This is the version of the thought group that might have been produced as an unmarked statement. However, alternative pronunciations are possible since the rhythm system is flexible and speakers are agents of rhythm. To convey a slightly different effect, a speaker might have decided to guide listeners' attentions to two rather than just a single prominent word, as in Figure 9.

In Figure 9 we see that prominence may be placed on more than one word in a thought group. Where prominence falls and the number of prominent locations are up to the speaker within the normal semantic and pragmatic constraints of English (see also Chapter 6). We could imagine a scenario in which some other word might be prominent. If, for example, the speaker's conversational partner had previously voiced the opinion that a doorway is something to be avoided during earthquakes, then the speaker might reply with an explicit contradiction (Figure 10).

Figure 8   // my mother says a DOORway is the safest //
(one thought group, one prominent word)

3	2	1
my mother says a	**DOOR**	way is the safest place

Figure 9   // my MOTHer says a DOORway is the safest place //
(one thought group, two prominent words)

5	4	3	2	1
my	**MOTH**	er says a	**DOOR**	way is the safest place

Figure 10   // my mother says a doorway is the SAFest place //

3	2	1
my mother says a doorway is the	**SAFE**	est place

Figure 11	// MY mother says a doorway is the SAFest place //		
4	3	2	1
My	mother says a doorway is the	**SAFE**	est place

Or an even more personalized effect be accomplished with the use of two, rather than just one, prominent words (Figure 11).

Figure 11 shows a subtly different application of prominence, perhaps used to imply the superiority of one mother's recommendation over another mother's recommendation.

A pivotal listening-pronunciation connection beyond the role of speaker agency is the high degree of compression of syllables, consonants, and vowels in thought group segments that happen to be non-prominent. In Figures 9, 10, and 11, for example, everything that appears in the odd-numbered columns 5, 3, and 1 is non-prominent and highly susceptible to the compression of phonological detail. For example, the non-prominent six-word segment situated between prominent words in Figure 11's column #3 (. . . mother says a doorway is the . . .) would likely be produced by an native speaker as not much more than a "difficult-for-ESL-listeners-to-interpret" mumble coinciding with multiple phonemic compressions and other naturally occurring phonological changes. An important yet often neglected goal of listening-pronunciation instruction is to build ESL listeners' awareness of just how normal and frequent it is for native language (L1) speakers to suppress phonological information in such non-prominent thought group segments. By building their awareness, ESL listeners can learn to recognize and anticipate the very high incidence and locations of such compression phenomena.

Conclusion

Along with calling for increased attention to the process of thought grouping, a dichotomy featured in this chapter is qualitative acoustic differences between prominent segments (PSs) and non-prominent segments (NPSs) of thought groups in spoken English. PSs are more salient, are more clearly enunciated, contain just one syllable, are easier for listeners to hear and distinguish, resist the suppression of phonological detail, and have traditionally served as the centerpiece of ESL listening-for-comprehension and fluency instruction. Although NPSs are less commonly taught in classrooms and considerably more difficult for ESL learners to hear and notice, their role is essential for a different set of ESL instructional purposes. NPSs may serve as centerpieces for form-focused, process-focused, listening-for-accuracy, *listening-to-be-able-to-understand-fast-fluent-L1-speech,* and *listening-for-the-mastery-of-linguistic-detail* instruction (see Cauldwell, 2013; Field 2008). As such, NPSs reside at the intersection of listening-pronunciation teaching. Though by no means comprehensive, what follows is a bullet list of some characteristics of non-prominent thought group segments (i.e., NPSs) accompanied by suggestions for classroom teaching. Activities such as these may be used along with the thought group listening discrimination and identification tasks presented earlier.

- NPSs are non-salient and indistinct in the stream of L1 speech.

- They occupy a larger portion of most thought groups and commonly contain multiple syllables.

- NPSs are more quickly pronounced (more syllables per second), with a decrease in volume and intensity.

- NPSs contribute rhythmically by occupying compressed spaces between spoken beats.

- Their compression of phonetic detail is normal, pervasive, and usually goes unnoticed.

- An increase in speaking tempo is normally accompanied by even more suppressions of phonological detail.

- In more formal situations (e.g., when speech is slower), NPSs may be clearer with fewer compressions.

Scavenger Hunt Activity

Exposing students to authentic samples of naturalistic discourse can illustrate just how pervasive NPSs are. An awareness-raising activity is a scavenger hunt in which students search on the Internet for video recordings of unrehearsed conversations between native (and other highly proficient) English speakers. Part of the students' charge is to locate brief segments in recordings they found to be decipherable only after repeated listening attempts. Eventually students introduce these segments to the class while discussing their listening difficulties along with any emerging compensation strategies. For more advanced-proficiency learners, corpus tools that provide sets of audio recordings paired with written transcripts. (e.g., Corpus of Contemporary American English, Michigan Corpus of Academic Spoken English, Santa Barbara Corpus of Spoken American English) can be used to support such tasks. At lower proficiency levels, sometimes just as useful are scenes from favorite movies and broadcast interviews.

Compressed Speech Activity

Through both listening recognition and pronunciation tasks, students can work with high-frequency stretches of speech that are often highly compressed. Students can practice listening for, and then producing, such stretches in both highly formalized (carefully enunciated) versions and highly compressed versions featuring phonological reductions/compressions. Here are some illustrations of speech samples to use in class when embedded within longer stretches of discourse:

FULL VERSION	HIGHLY COMPRESSED VERSION
What did you eat for lunch?	/wədžiyfərləntš/
What is the matter?	/smædər/
How did you do on the test?	/hadžəduwənðətest/
I have got to go.	/aygədəgow/
See you later.	/leydər/
It is all over.	/tsɔlowvər/

Related discussion can focus on which parts (e.g., syllables) are maintained and which become obscured in fast fluent speech. For added practice, students can be asked to design practice scenarios in which these phrases might appear (i.e., one such dialogue for each phrase).

Undergraduate Questions Activity

The University of Minnesota's Center for Teaching and Learning makes available an Internet resource titled *Common Questions for International TAs.*[6] This audio resource is designed to provide international teaching assistants with opportunities to listen to, guess at the meaning of, and then read a series of questions that undergraduate students typically ask in class. The site provides over 150 such questions. Examples include highly compressed versions of undergrad students' queries: "How long's the test gonna be?" "What (did) I do wrong here?" "You shoulda told us this was gonna be on the test." "I really messed up on this one." "How come our answers are exactly the same but I got two points off and he got full credit?" This resource can be used to provide listening practice in the identification of thought groups, consonant deletions, assimilations, and other naturally occurring phonological changes characteristic of fast fluent speech. Following listening analysis, it can also be used as a model for pronunciation practice.

---

6 http://www1.umn.edu/ohr//teachlearn/graduate/itap/nonnative/questions/index.html.

Variation-in-Pronunciation Activity

Whenever teaching new vocabulary or responding to students' questions about the pronunciation of a particular word, always teach the word's full citation form (the clear form of pronunciation when the word is prominent within a thought group), but also teach at least one of the less distinct forms the same word takes when it is located within a thought group's non-prominent segment. A word's citation form is what ESL learners may expect to hear, but non-prominent forms are what they are likely to hear more often. When teaching such variations in the pronunciation of particular vocabulary, illustrations need to be embedded within thought groups to be able to call learners' attention to connections between speech rhythms, prominence, and pronunciation. The following three-line dialogue illustrates a citation form of the word *psychological* as it would occur in a prominent thought group location and then a non-prominent form of the same word at its second mention in the dialogue:

A: What kind of a problem does he have?

B: He has a PSYcho**LOG**ical problem.

It's a very se**VERE** psychological problem.

The speaker's first version of *psychological* would likely be pronounced as a five-syllable word with primary stress on the third syllable (and secondary stress on the first syllable). This is the word's citation form; its thought group may be depicted as:

3	2	1
he has a psycho	**LOG**	ical problem

In contrast, the next thought group features the newly introduced (and prominent) adjective *severe* immediately followed by what would now have become a non-prominent version of *psychological*. Since this second mention of *psychological* is non-prominent, the word would likely be reduced from five to just four syllables, with the vowel of what was its second syllable in citation form (i.e., *cho*) likely suppressed.

3	2	1
it's a very se	**VERE**	psychological problem

In fact, in the speech of many native speakers, when *psychological* is non-prominent its entire second syllable (i.e., *cho*) might be deleted. Further, in an even more compressed fast-speech version, *psychological* might be as extremely compressed as a three-syllable *sLOGical*. Just as these analyses of alternative pronunciations move us quite far from the word's citation form, they remind us of the impossible-to-ignore interplay between thought groups, prominence, variations in pronunciation, and listeners' expectations. As listeners, ESL students need to anticipate and learn to expect variations in pronunciation as conditioned by prominence locations. A central function of listening-pronunciation practice is to support students as they learn to listen for, and to decipher, both the citation and non-prominent forms of whatever vocabulary they are learning.

> **Disappearing Text Activity**
>
> Dictation, cloze, and dicto-comp tasks can all provide ESL students with listening practice focused on non-prominent spans of speech. Dicto-comp begins as a standard dictation activity. Once students have produced their initial versions, they then collaborate by taking turns saying the text aloud for one or more peers until, collaboratively, they succeed in reconstructing a complete version. Marks and Bowen (2012) describe a modification they call "disappearing text" (p. 94) in which listeners are provided with successive (e.g., four to five) written versions of a single 80- to 100-word oral text. Each subsequent version presented has a few more of the non-prominent sections deleted. For each round, the teacher presents the oral version once while listeners attempt to fill in the increasing number of gaps in each printed version. For a final round, the largest number of sections are deleted and can be tailored to focus learners' attention specifically on non-prominent components of the speech signal.

- NPSs function more as carriers of linguistic (syntactic, phonological) detail, less as carriers of new substantive content information.

- ESL listeners find it difficult to make sense of NPSs during dictation exercises; therefore, for purpose of listening for the master of linguistic detail, they may benefit from such practice.

Cauldwell (2013, pp. 317–320) provides practical guidelines for any English speakers interested in learning to be able to compress the phonological detail of NPSs in naturalistic ways. To illustrate such connections between listening and pronunciation, teachers might share Cauldwell's guidelines with ESL learners as a valuable resource for enhancing their ability to recognize and make sense of such naturally occurring characteristic of English speech. Field (2008) provides a book-length discussion of why phonological compressions in NPSs are essential to include when teaching the process of L2 listening. Both of these innovative books, though focused on the process of L2 listening, may be read to inform more integrated ESL instruction in listening and pronunciation.

References

Cauldwell, R. (2000). The functional irrhythmicality of spontaneous speech: A discourse view of speech rhythms. *Apples, 2*(1), 1–24.

Cauldwell, R. (2002). *Streaming speech: Listening and pronunciation for advanced learners of English* [CD-ROM]. Birmingham, England: Speech in Action.

Cauldwell, R. (2013). *Phonology for listening: Teaching the stream of speech.* Birmingham, England: Speech in Action.

Dickerson, W. (2010). Walking the walk: Integrating the story of English phonology. In J. M. Levis & K. LeVelle (Eds.), *Proceedings of the 1st pronunciation in second language learning and teaching conference* (pp. 10–23). Ames: Iowa State University.

ESL dialogue: Earthquake! (2012). Retrieved from http://www.stickyball.net/dialogues.html?id=217

Field, J. (2008). *Listening and the language classroom.* New York, NY: Cambridge University Press.

Gilbert, J. B. (2008). *Teaching pronunciation: Using the prosody pyramid.* Cambridge, England: Cambridge University Press.

Koch, A. (n.d.). *Science vocabulary and concepts: Study skills and word parts.* Retrieved from http://education-portal.com/academy/lesson/science-vocabulary-concepts-study-skills-word-parts.html#lesson

Lane, L. (2010). *Tips for teaching pronunciation: A practical approach.* White Plains, NY: Pearson/Longman.

Marks, J., & Bowen, T. (2012). *The book of pronunciation.* Surrey, England: Delta.

Murphy, J. (2013). *Teaching pronunciation.* Alexandria, VA: TESOL International Association.

O'Keeffe, A., McCarthy, M., & Carter, R. (2007). *From corpus to classroom.* Cambridge, England: Cambridge University Press.

Wong, R. (1987). *Teaching pronunciation: Focus on English rhythm and intonation.* Englewood Cliffs, NJ: Prentice Hall Regents.

CHAPTER 6

Pronunciation, Stress and Intonation, and Communicative Listening Skills

Marnie Reed

Learners of English face two listening challenges: development of parsing skills necessary to understand the ostensible meaning of an utterance, the locution, and inferencing skills necessary to interpret a speaker's intended or implied meaning, the illocutionary force of an utterance.[1] Helping learners understand the locution, the actual utterance, requires addressing factors that impact second language (L2) segmentation of rapid continuous discourse (see Chapter 5). These factors include cross-linguistic differences in word-boundary acoustic cues (Altenberg, 2005) as well as overreliance on native processing strategies for word recognition and segmentation (Field, 2008). However, helping learners understand the illocutionary force of an utterance, the topic of this chapter, requires addressing factors that contribute to pragmatic inference in English. This presents a different and perhaps more formidable challenge in that "often what a speaker intends to say is not always directly retrievable from a linguistic form: rather listeners must infer it" (Tomlinson & Bott, 2013, p. 3569). This may be why, as noted by Vandergrift and Goh (2012), learners who have reached a threshold level of proficiency sufficient to segment words in connected speech nevertheless report difficulties with inferences, specifically, "understanding the words but not the message" (p. 22).

To illustrate the locution/illocution distinction, consider the two sentences below:

Example 1

(a) My boss said he'd fixed all the problems.
(b) My boss *said* he'd fixed all the problems.

---

[1] The theoretical framework for this chapter on the implicational function of intonation is speech act theory (Austin, 1962; Searle, 1969).

Sentence (a) is a relatively straightforward case of reported speech; none of the lexical items is likely to pose difficulties for students, especially at intermediate to advanced levels. In order to understand it, L2 learners of English require competence with aural processing skills, including phonotactics of the permissible sequence of sounds to parse or segment, and ability to decode connected speech features. This sentence presents instances of linked sounds (*said he'd* and *fixed all*), contracted sounds (*he'd*), deleted sounds (~~he~~'d), and grammar sounds, in this case knowledge that the pronunciation of the regular past participle verb is one syllable, /fɪkst/ (not /fɪk sEd/). Sentence (b), on the other hand, is no longer a case of reported speech. The use of italics in print cancels the neutral interpretation; it highlights the selected word, giving it prominence and requiring a different, marked interpretation. The information signaled by italics on the printed page (i.e., which word receives focus or prominence) is signaled orally by stress and intonation, specifically, by the "implicational fall-rise" pitch contour superimposed on the vowel in *said* to indicate "the speaker implies something without necessarily putting it into words" (Wells, 2006, p. 27). Learners whose overall impression of English is that its normal stress patterns are exaggerated may be insensitive to the way that native speakers use stress and intonation as devices to draw attention to what is implied but left unstated.

Stress and intonation are among the suprasegmental, or prosodic, elements of pronunciation—that is, information that rides above the level of the individual consonant and vowel segments, the elements that learners often perceive to be their greatest pronunciation problems. According to Gilbert (2014), "prosodic cues serve as navigation guides to help the listener follow the intentions of the speaker" (p. 123). Wells (2006) defines intonation as "the rise and fall of pitch in our voices [that] plays a crucial role in how we express meaning" (p. i). He goes on to point out that "it well may be the case that English makes more elaborate use of intonation to signal meaning than do most other languages" but also observes that "the native speaker, unaware both of his or her own use of intonation and of the non-native's failure to pick up on it, wrongly assumes that the message has been fully understood" (Wells, 2006, p. 11). This observation suggests a metacognitive gap on the part of both the native and the nonnative speaker, a gap that has also been noted by Grant (2014), who writes that "native speakers use suprasegmental features unconsciously. Like their students, native-speaking teachers are seldom aware of speech features like English rhythm and intonation and how they impact meaning unless those concepts are explicitly pointed out" (pp. 13–14). It is important, therefore, to establish for our learners an appreciation of the normal, albeit "elaborate," intonation contours of English phrases and sentences as a foundation for recognition, and ultimately interpretation, of intonation contours that are used for pragmatic effect. Otherwise, as Gilbert warns, learners "may think that intonation is simply decorative" (p. 125).

Among the pragmatic functions of intonation that native speakers and learners alike may be unaware of is its illocutionary "power to reinforce, mitigate, or even undermine the words spoken" (Wichmann, 2005, p. 229).

This chapter aims to increase learner and instructor awareness of the communicative role of intonation and the importance of listening for what is meant. As Brown (2011) asserts, "listeners must listen strategically" (p. 80). A logical starting place for awareness raising is the learner beliefs that underpin the approaches they take to second language listening, since "learner beliefs affect the range of language learning strategies employed and also affect the motivation to learn, thereby indirectly influencing L2 learning outcomes" (Nix & Tseng, 2014, p. 114). To fall short of our awareness-raising objective would leave us in the untenable situation described by Paunović and Savić (2008) in which

> students often do not have a clear idea of why exactly 'the melody of speech' should be important for communication, and therefore seem to lack the motivation to master it, while teachers do not seem to be theoretically or practically well-equipped to explain and illustrate its significance. (pp. 72–73)

Learners who have taken or prepared to take various tests of English language proficiency, such as the TOEFL or IELTS, are likely to already be familiar with making inferences when reading, as this is among the reading skills typically included in these assessments. Learners may be less familiar with the prosodic indicators in spoken English that require making inferences, relying instead on lexis or syntax rather than intonation to process aural input. The task of sentence inferencing when listening—the task of determining a speaker's intended meaning and in many cases anticipating what will be said next—entails first the aural detection that an utterance is deviating from the neutral, unmarked stress and intonation of English as well as recognition that the speaker is employing—to use Pickering's (2012) definition of intonation—"linguistically meaningful use of pitch movement at the phrasal or suprasegmental level" (p. 280) to go beyond the literal meaning of the utterance. Since adult learners of English are generally reported not to spontaneously acquire its prosody, or to do so only at advanced stages of acquisition (Ioup & Tansomboon, 1987), this recognition must come primarily through effective pronunciation instruction that targets both productive and metacognitive levels. In other words, in order to prepare learners to draw on intonation when interpreting speakers' meanings, we must follow the advice of Allen (1971), who advocated instruction that "teaches the student to think in terms of the speaker's intention in any given situation" (p. 73).

With this advice in mind, it seems reasonable to advocate explicit listening instruction that first acknowledges that the normal prosody of English is already more elaborate than what many of the world's languages employ to convey normal unmarked meaning. With an established baseline of "elaborate" English prosody as comparable to other languages' neutral prosody, the instructional task broadens to encompass the even greater pitch ranges that English employs to convey new or contrastive information, emphasis, or unspoken but intended implications. Haugh (2002) noted that "the most crucial characteristic of *implying* and thus implicature, is that it involves something which is meant *in addition* to what is literally said" (p. 130, italics in original). Keeping in mind Wells's (2006) characterization of normal English intonation as "elaborate," it would seem that for our purposes, the term *implicational intonation* can be adopted to capture the marked or enhanced intonation contours that signal what the speaker intends to imply and the listener must infer. It is these marked implicational stress and intonation patterns that play key roles in helping listeners disambiguate a message and truly understand a speaker's illocutionary force. Therefore, pronunciation instruction that is added to listening lessons—or any lesson in which listening is one of the key goals—needs to focus not only on the normal phrase-level and sentence-level stress and intonation patterns of English pronunciation but on implicational intonation as well. This is good news for teachers who are teaching listening—it sharpens the instructional focus of pronunciation into a manageable task that truly complements listening instruction.

Three Key Connections From Pronunciation to Listening for the Illocutionary Force

1. In English, implicational intonation can override the words of utterances; that is, stress and intonation can change the meaning of the utterance in a sentence and add an implication.

2. Learners who haven't had practice producing these kinds of marked stress and intonation patterns may not be able to hear them at all (skill-based side).

3. Learners who haven't grappled with the pragmatic functions of intonation may be able to hear marked intonation/stress but not pick up on the added implications (metacognitive side).

Therefore, instruction in marked, implicational intonation and stress for the purposes of helping with listening for the illocution, the speaker's intended meaning, must proceed along two levels—the skill level and the metacognitive level—for learners to be successful listeners.

Applications for Practice

Many listening textbooks or integrated skills books that include listening sections contain pronunciation topics along with listening tasks. However, often these pronunciation topics are tangentially related, at best, to helping learners with the actual listening task. Pronunciation sections often target connected speech features such as reductions and linking, features of English that are important for decoding spoken content, the locution. In order to aid listening for speaker intent, the illocution, pronunciation sections focused on contrastive stress and implicational intonation must be included as well. Where these are lacking, lessons can be supplemented with more emphasis on suprasegmentals earlier in the course (see Reed, 2014).

Unfortunately, when instructors turn to curriculum guidelines in order to advance learner knowledge and control of listening processes, they often discover objectives that are not operationalized. The thrust of many intermediate- to advanced-level listening classes, especially in the context of intensive English programs, is to prepare students to listen to academic lectures in English. Institutional goals such as "Students will be able to comprehend lectures and engage in academic conversation" typically leave the task of operationalizing these goals to instructors, without providing instructors with the means to teach the skills and to assess whether students have attained them at the metacognitive and procedural levels. As a result, most listening "instruction" does not actually teach students how to listen—that is, it does not equip learners with the necessary concepts and scaffold them in their use in order to process the listening input. Much of this type of listening instruction either relies on a listening "comprehension" approach that parallels reading comprehension instruction, ignoring the specific aural nature of the activity, or bypasses instruction entirely and simply tests listening ability. As Mendelsohn (2006) cautioned, "much of what is traditionally mis-named *teaching* listening should in fact be called *testing* listening" (p. 75, italics in original). It's true that listening to lectures does involve some attention to discourse-specific features such as transitional elements, signaling phrases (*first, next*, etc.), and other oral/aural elements parallel to those involved in the process of reading comprehension. However, effective listening instruction has to require students to decode and make sense of the aural information and process it appropriately.

This processing, and therefore listening instruction, functions at two levels. Recalling Example 1, we saw that understanding the locution required knowledge of phonotactic constraints and connected speech features. In order to move to the level of understanding the illocutionary force of this utterance, though, learners must understand all of the above plus the pragmatic functions of the implicational intonation in this context, which changes the utterance from a case of reported speech

into an opinion-based commentary on the speaker's boss. The production, pragmatics, and metacognition of intonation and stress, therefore, are key to helping
learners correctly make sense of this statement. Even in listening or integrated skills
courses that are aimed at equipping learners to understand academic lectures, then,
pronunciation instruction has to begin at the level of the utterance, not at the larger
discourse level. Teachers can therefore continue to use academic lectures as assessment, periodically throughout the semester and at the end of the course, but actual
instruction should use standard conversational contexts and activities to prepare
students to apply their knowledge of suprasegmental features and their pragmatic
functions to eventually understanding academic lectures.

Another strategy that listening textbooks often use is prompting learners to listen for key words when trying to focus on the main ideas. This seems like a useful
strategy, but two problems occur. First of all, due to the reductions and other aspects
characteristic of connected speech, learners may hear the key words (the unreduced
content words) correctly but miss the reduced, altered, and other types of function
words and may therefore miss the entire locution itself (see Chapter 5). More important for our purposes here, when discussing intonation, function words sometimes
receive nonstandard stress and intonation in utterances, particularly in cases when
they are so important that they change the meaning of the utterance. In both cases,
though, learners are focusing exclusively on words (semantics—word meanings and
locution), rather than on the illocution, or message meaning.

Most listening instruction begins by having learners attend closely to what they
actually hear—the sound level, the acoustic signal. As explained above, the acoustic
signal alone doesn't help learners, so we teach them the sound signal distortion
patterns, connected speech features, and they move another step closer to comprehension; they are now able to discern individual words and segment the speech
stream—that is, they can understand the locution. However, they cannot stop here;
they must grasp the suprasegmental concepts that are key to expressing meaning.
With knowledge of implicational stress and intonation, then, learners can finally
understand the illocution. Instruction to foster this understanding can start with
reading passages in which illocutionary force is conveyed through the device of
italicized words. Since read-aloud is a frequent classroom activity, students can be
instructed to scan passages for words in italics and articulate their findings. Examples
of these abound, as we discover once we are sensitive to the need to provide samples
for practice. On the topic of the influence of language on determining how we see
the world, for instance, an article in *The New York Times* (Deutscher, 2010) quoted
linguist Roman Jakobson: "Languages differ essentially in what they *must* convey and
not in what they *may* convey." The *Times* author expounds on the passage, offering
two additional italicized words in his discussion of this claim. While read-aloud is

not a recognized reading skill, we can nevertheless benefit from its diagnostic utility in revealing learner treatment, which is typically to read the italicized words no differently from the way they read words not in italics.

Returning to sentence (b) in Example 1, we can present the sentence first in a reading passage—"My boss *said* he'd fixed all the problems"—and elicit the observation, "The word *said* is in italics." Next, we can elicit student tell-backs, statements that mirror the original language of instruction. For example, learners should be able to restate the concept "Words in italics signal special meaning, such as contrasts or implications." Building on the metacognitive foundation that italics signal a marked interpretation, move to the procedural level for oral production. Introduce the implicational fall-rise pitch contour, bearing in mind that while students may reject adoption of this extra "elaborate" intonation, they must nevertheless be able to detect and interpret it in listening input. It can also be informative for learners to be assigned to solicit a reading of this sentence and interpretation of its meaning from a fixed number of native speakers, then report their findings at the next class meeting. The fact that native speakers listening to sentence (a) in Example 1 will assume the problems have been fixed, while those listening to sentence (b) will not, based solely on implicational intonation (or the use of italics in print), is often an eye-opener for learners, while learner failure to reach this interpretation is equally eye-opening for teachers.

Example 2

Student, seeking feedback after an oral presentation: How was my analysis? Teacher: Well, you gave a good *summary*.

In this case, the teacher's words are positive and affirming, but the message is not. Learners who are not used to attending to implicational intonation may respond happily, thinking their presentation was successful, when in fact the teacher's implication was that the student's analysis (presumably the point of the presentation) was lacking.

Learners who entirely miss the important implication of an utterance are in great need of help. Situations arise frequently in classrooms when students seek affirmative feedback, as in Example 2, or request permission (e.g., "Can I turn in my assignment late?") or advice (e.g., "Is it okay to skip the field trip?"). These often elicit teacher responses that seem positive (e.g., "You *can*," "You *could*") but with implicational intonation that overrides the lexical denotation. Feedback in the form of repetition, discussed in the Additional Benefits section later in the chapter, is another situation in which teachers risk mistakenly assuming that the pitch change they employ to highlight erroneous elements in learners' speech will be recognized as an error correction. Empirical evidence (Lyster & Ranta, 1997, p. 54) and teachers' own experience compel us to consider that unless learners can detect intonation that deviates from the norm and grasp its signaling function, this form of feedback will not lead to successful repair. Thus, teaching intonation helps learners when listening for important implications—in other words, when inferring speaker intent.

Next, extend instruction of marked, implicational intonation and contrastive stress to sentences with no equivalent use of italics in print. A set of quotations in the Words of Wisdom section of Grant's (2001, p. 107) *Well Said* provides opportunities for awareness raising and practice. Learners can be guided to find the contrastive words or elements, for example, the prepositions in "Whoever gossips to you will gossip about you," and predict and practice the intonation contour. This is another case in which it can be instructive to have learners listen for and verify the use of marked intonation by native speakers in a random sample.

Example 3

Given the sound file, "The *teacher* didn't grade your papers," subjects in a recent study overwhelmingly believed the papers had not been graded.

When hearing statements like that in Example 3, learners are likely to rely on the locution—the words—to make sense of the speaker's meaning. As Reed and Michaud (2015) report, learners attended to the words *didn't grade* in the middle of the sentence, and when asked the question, "Have the papers been graded?" they relied on those words to answer in the negative. Native speaker listeners hearing the same sentence, on the other hand, with the same implicational stress and intonation on *teacher*, pick up on the important implication that, yes, the papers have been graded—but presumably by someone other than the teacher, perhaps a teaching assistant. In this case, consistent with Wichmann's (2005) claim that the intonation can trump the words, learners' failure to pick up on the pragmatic function of implicational stress and intonation leads them to make factual errors. This is a real-world, potentially serious effect that highlights the importance of intonation and can be eye-opening to both teachers and learners. A Teaching Tip recommended by Reed (2014, p. 199) is to introduce an implicational checklist to assess aural discrimination and ability to make inferences. The checklist requires the following: detection of similarity or difference in a forced choice task (Do samples 1 and 2—neutral, unmarked intonation versus marked, implicational intonation—sound the same or different?), identification of implicational intonation as the differentiating factor (the word *teacher* had implicational intonation), and a plausible inference (someone else graded the papers, not the teacher).

Example 4

"Let's conTINnue our disCUSsion of polLUtion. YESterday we deFINED

pollution. ToDAY we'll talk about the IMpact of pollution." (Grant, 2001, p. 97)

In this example, in the context of a longer lecture, the superscripted dots show the words that receive prominence or focus in each sentence. It's possible to trace the thread of the speaker's focus through these three sentences on two levels—both using intonation and using the speaker's words themselves, with the first sentence functioning as a topic sentence giving listeners clues about what will follow. However, we can see the importance of intonation itself, above and beyond the words, if we ignore, for the moment, the first sentence; if someone arrived late, for example, and heard only the second sentence, he or she would still know that the topic is pollution, and the next utterance would expand on that same topic rather than move on to a new topic. Therefore, even in the absence of topic sentences that explicitly signal the topic, intonation helps listeners predict which discoursal path the speaker will take: expanding on the current topic or introducing a new one.

Example 5

(a) In our unit on social media we've been discussing the invention of Facebook.
(b) Next we'll talk about the impact of Facebook.

Example 6

(a) In our unit on social media we've been discussing the invention of Facebook.
(b) Next we'll talk about the invention of Twitter.

Whereas the wide pitch range English employs in Example 5 highlights contrasting elements—something about X, something else about X—the equivalent pitch range in Example 6 signals given versus new information: something about X, something about Y. Bearing in mind Gilbert's (2014) caution that "students will rarely tell the teacher that they feel silly speaking this way" (p. 125), instruction must move beyond mere student imitation of the target stress and intonation to addressing the functions these pitch movements serve. Student tell-backs both promote and reveal learner metacognition, for example, "We need extra stress and intonation on the words *invention* and *impact* because they're contrastive." A strategy-based metacognitive approach to listening instruction that requires learners to articulate the communicative and pragmatic functions of contrastive stress and implicational intonation can promote both the awareness and skill proficiency necessary to infer speakers' intended meaning.

Example 7

Some companies in the tech sector sell a wide variety of products.

In the pilot study cited by Reed and Michaud (2015), advanced-level students achieved near-native intonation in a language lab session following intensive coaching on the sentence in Example 7. When listening to that sentence in the following lab session, however, they were unable to use intonation to accurately identify the likely topic of the next sentence. Their confidence in sentence position to privilege the "wide variety of products" was sufficiently strong to challenge the assertion that native speakers hearing the same sentence would be alerted on the basis of the marked intonation on *some* to hearing about other companies instead. Learners need to be explicitly taught both the production of this kind of sentence-level intonation and stress and also the pragmatics of it—in other words, its important predictive power. (See Chapters 3, 4, 5, and 7 for suggestions for more practice activities for prominence.)

Additional Benefits of Intonation Instruction for Listening

Teaching suprasegmental pronunciation topics such as intonation has additional benefits for learners and can aid them in everyday classroom communicative contexts, to help learners both troubleshoot their own communication breakdowns and make sense of teacher corrective feedback.

Many listening books coach learners in strategies designed to help with communication breakdowns, suggesting, among other things, that learners pay attention to their interlocutor's paralinguistics, looking for furrowed brows and other signs of puzzlement. These strategies are useful when communication breakdowns do occur, but teaching contrastive stress and marked, implicational intonation can help learners avoid communication breakdowns by giving them more ways to make sense of an utterance rather than just relying on a speaker's words. Furthermore, when communication breakdowns do occur, learners can be taught to ask short, focused questions with a specific rising intonation contour in order to elicit the specific information they need clarification on, rather than a general repeat or recast of the utterance.

Example 8

Teacher: Open your book to page <mumble>.
Student: Page what? (Reed & Michaud, 2005, p. 167)

As noted above, teachers unconsciously use implicational intonation all the time in the classroom, often using repetition or recasts as forms of corrective feedback. In describing treatment of errors, his preferred term for corrective feedback, Chaudron (1977) specified a category of "repetition with change and emphasis" (p. 39), and Lyster and Ranta's (1997) classification of "repetition" includes this note: "In most cases, teachers adjust their intonation so as to highlight the error" (p. 48). Teachers believe the marked intonation highlights the specific part of the utterance that has an error, but learners often fail to notice the intonation contour and treat the teacher's prompt either as a simple clarification request or as conversational back-channeling. In the course of teaching students how to produce these intonation contours, we can highlight the pedagogical function that they have in this context, so that learners will be better able to make sense of teachers' feedback.

Conclusions

Pronunciation instruction is key to successful listening ability, a connection that both teachers and learners may find quite surprising. Teaching specific suprasegmental pronunciation features can promote successful sentence inferencing in listening contexts. Teachers who approach the teaching of listening in the ways advocated in this chapter may find themselves undergoing an important mental shift: Instead of thinking of themselves as teaching listening, and adding some pronunciation topics as extras, they may begin to see themselves as teaching intonation in order to directly improve learners' abilities to listen for what is meant. Intonation therefore becomes essential for success in the context of the listening classroom. Even teachers who work in programs where the listening objectives are vague and not operationalized (e.g., "Students will understand lectures") will now be able to define for themselves—and more important, for their learners—the specific intonation concepts and patterns that learners must master in order to understand what is meant by what is said.

References

Allen, V. (1971). Teaching intonation, from theory to practice. *TESOL Quarterly, 4,* 73–81.

Altenberg, E. P. (2005). The perception of word boundaries in a second language. *Second Language Research, 21,* 325–358.

Austin, J. (1962). *How to do things with words* (2nd ed.). Cambridge, MA: Harvard University Press.

Brown, S. (2011). *Listening myths: Applying second language research to classroom teaching*. Ann Arbor: University of Michigan Press.

Chaudron, C. (1977). A descriptive model of discourse in the corrective treatment of learners' errors. *Language Learning, 27*(1), 29–46.

Deutscher, G. (2010, August 26). Does your language shape how you think? *New York Times*.

Field, J. (2008). Revising segmentation hypotheses in first and second language listening. *System, 36*, 35–51.

Gilbert, J. (2014). Myth 4: Intonation is hard to teach. In L. Grant (Ed.), *Pronunciation myths: Applying second language research to classroom teaching* (pp. 107–136). Ann Arbor: University of Michigan Press.

Grant, L. (2001). *Well said: Pronunciation for clear communication* (2nd ed.). Boston, MA: Heinle & Heinle.

Grant, L. (2014). Prologue to the myths: What teachers need to know. In L. Grant (Ed.), *Pronunciation myths: Applying second language research to classroom teaching* (pp. 1–33). Ann Arbor: University of Michigan Press.

Haugh, M. (2002). The intuitive basis of implicature: Relevance theoretical *implicitness* versus Gricean *implying*. *Pragmatics, 12*(2), 117–134.

Ioup, G., & Tansomboon, A. (1987). The acquisition of tone: A maturational perspective. In G. Ioup & S. Weinberger (Eds.), *International phonology: The acquisition of a second language sound system* (pp. 333–349). New York, NY: Newbury House/Harper & Row.

Lyster, R., & Ranta, L. (1997). Corrective feedback and learner uptake: Negotiation of form in communicative classrooms. *Studies in Second Language Acquisition, 20*, 37–66.

Mendelsohn, D. (2006). Learning how to listen using learning strategies. In P. Gorden (Ed.), *Current trends in the development and teaching of the four language skills* (pp. 75–89). Berlin, Germany: Mouton de Gruyter.

Nix, J.-M. L, & Tseng, W.-T. (2014). Towards the measurement of EFL listening beliefs with item response theory methods. *International Journal of Listening, 28*, 112–130.

Paunović, T., & Savić, M. (2008). Discourse intonation—Making it work. In S. Komar & U. Mozetič (Eds.), *As you write it: Issues in literature, language, and translation in the context of Europe in the 21st century, V*(1–2), 57–75. Ljubljana, Slovenia: Slovene Association for the Study of English.

Pickering, L. (2012). Intonation. In K. Malmkjaer (Ed.), *The Routledge linguistics encyclopedia* (3rd ed., pp. 280–286). New York, NY: Routledge.

Reed, M. (2014). The English syllable: Big news, bad news and its importance for intelligibility. In J. Levis & S. McCrocklin (Eds.), *Proceedings of the 5th Pronunciation in Second Language Learning and Teaching Conference* (pp. 189–202). Ames: Iowa State University.

Reed, M., & Michaud, C. (2005). *Sound concepts: An integrated pronunciation course*. New York, NY: McGraw-Hill.

Reed, M., & Michaud, C. (2015). Intonation in research and practice: The importance of metacognition. In M. Reed & J. Levis (Eds.), *The handbook of English pronunciation* (pp. 454–470). Malden, MA: Wiley Blackwell.

Searle, J. (1969). *Speech acts.* New York, NY: Cambridge University Press.

Tomlinson, J. M., & Bott, L. (2013). How intonation constrains pragmatic inference. In M. Knauff, M. Pauen, N. Sebanz, & I. Wachsmuth (Eds.), *Proceedings of the 35th Annual Conference of the Cognitive Science Society* (pp. 3569–3574). Austin, TX: Cognitive Science Society.

Vandergrift, L., & Goh, C. (2012). *Teaching and learning second language listening: Metacognition in action.* New York, NY: Routledge.

Wells, J. C. (2006). *English intonation: An introduction.* Cambridge, England: Cambridge University Press.

Wichmann, A. (2005). Please—from courtesy to appeal: The role of intonation in the expression of attitudinal meaning. *English Language and Linguistics, 9,* 229–253.

CHAPTER 7

Taking the Fear Factor Out of Integrating Pronunciation and Beginning Grammar

Sue F. Miller and Tamara Jones

As English spreads across the globe, emerging markets for new English speakers demand good oral communications skills, including clear pronunciation. While teachers of beginning grammar classes encounter the same challenges as others who wish to integrate pronunciation into their class work, they also face the difficulty of making a complex subject accessible to their students. However, as Gilbert (2001) states, "surely it would be better to help [beginners] early, rather than wait until they have developed habits which must be undone" (p. 173). This leaves educators wondering how to integrate pronunciation into beginning grammar classes simply and effectively. What can we teach our students that will make the biggest difference in their speech? Is it possible to teach pronunciation from the beginning and integrate it into our classes as we teach grammar? If so, what can teachers focus on that will benefit their students the most?

The answers lie in the fact that improving prosody, or the musical flow of speech—emphasizing speech rhythm, stress, and intonation, rather than sounds—makes the biggest difference in a speaker's intelligibility. According to Derwing and Rossiter (2003), although individual sounds are important, prosody is primary. In fact, to improve pronunciation, the prosodic signals of English are the most important things a student can learn (Gilbert, 2008). Fortunately, pronunciation experts have discovered that a short list of high-priority features can make a huge difference in intelligibility. We call this list the *prosody package* and it includes the following core features of English pronunciation: word stress (the strongly stressed syllable), speech rhythm (strong and weak beats in a phrase), prominence (the strongest beat in each phrase or short sentence), linking (connecting words), speech or thought groups (short units of speech with one strong beat, separated by pauses), and intonation (speech melody/pitch changes).

Rather than approaching these core prosodic features as additions to the curriculum, pronunciation instruction can be viewed as integral to learning spoken grammar. Good verbal skills require both good grammar and clear speech, taught in tandem from the beginning. After all, what good are hours spent mastering grammar structures if no one can understand what the student is saying? When started early, students learn how to use these core features to speak English intelligibly as they learn the grammar. Furthermore, students master the grammar more easily and remember it better when they practice it orally using good prosody. Integrating pronunciation and grammar from the beginning can also help avert fossilization of incorrect patterns, often stemming from the student's original language patterns transferred to English.

The next sections offer suggestions about how to integrate teaching grammar along with the prosody package without creating new materials.

Integrating Pronunciation Into the Simple Present With *Be*

Several popular grammar series, including *Focus on Grammar* (Schoenburg & Maurer, 2012), *Basic English Grammar* (Azar & Hagen, 2014), and *Grammar Sense* (Pavlik, 2012), begin their lowest level texts with the verb *to be*, an excellent place to start integrating prosody and grammar. This sentence practice in *Basic English Grammar* asks students to complete sentences with nouns.

A bird is <u>an animal</u>.

Tennis is <u>a sport.</u>

Chicago is <u>a city</u>.

Spanish is <u>a language</u>.

(Azar & Hagen, 2014, p. 9)

These simple sentences present several possibilities. Teachers could draw students' attention to the multisyllabic words and address word stress, as in chi**CA**go and **TENN**is, where one syllable is strongly stressed. Teachers could also point out how to link combinations of words like an **AN**imal, sounding like /nænəməl/. By having students keep the same rhythm while inserting new vocabulary, teachers can expand Azar and Hagen's activity. This repetition of a prosodic pattern is invaluable, especially for beginners.

As Gilbert (2001) cautions, "students can only deal with a limited number of challenges at one time" (p. 173). Therefore, rather than overwhelm students with detailed pronunciation rules, teachers can introduce English prosody using choral practice with the class and the teacher. Choral practice is an entertaining but also powerful tool for transmitting the rhythm of English speech, especially for beginners learning pronunciation (Kjellin, 1999). The teacher prompts students to listen first and then "Say it with me." This is different from "listen and repeat" because the sound of the teacher's voice is needed to carry the chorus of student voices along. Choral practice, accompanied by body movements, such as clapping and leaning forward on the strong beats, greatly increases the likelihood that students will internalize the pronunciation patterns of English.

In the following exercises practicing the simple present, these strong beats are shown in capital letters and bold type to illustrate prominence, or focus a key prosodic feature of English, where one word in each phrase or short sentence is strongly stressed (see Chapters 3 and 4). Students can chorally repeat sentences such as "You're very **NICE**" while clapping and leaning forward on the focus word *nice*. Here are a few other examples:

> I'm **LATE**. (clap)
>
> She's **HUN**gry. (clap)
>
> We're **STU**dents. (clap)
>
> (Azar & Hagen, 2014, p. 11)

Meyers and Holt (2001) describe another exercise using clapping to imprint prosody. Students start with two or three stressed words, clapping on each strong beat. Then they add unstressed words without changing the rhythm of the clapping. Notice in the following example that the last word gets the strongest stress, or focus.

> ICE (clap) SNOW (clap) **COLD** (clap)
>
> ICE (clap) and SNOW (clap) are **COLD** (clap)
>
> The ICE (clap) and SNOW (clap) are so **COLD** (clap)
>
> (Adapted from Azar & Hagen, 2014, p. 17)

Adding physical movements during choral practice helps students internalize prosodic patterns and use them in speech, whether students clap, tap a pencil, or nod their heads on the focus words (see Chapter 2). When new words are introduced, students can stretch a rubber band as they lengthen the stressed vowel sound, in either choral or conversational practice (Gilbert, 2008).

Many beginning grammar books talk about parts of speech. For example, Azar and Hagen (2014) introduce *to be* with a chart containing the terms *noun + noun: singular* and *article*. Teachers could point out that nouns and verbs are usually stressed, while articles are usually unstressed in English. This initiates the conversation about grammar and stress from the start.

Integrating Pronunciation and the Simple Present Tense

Using third person verbs in conversation presents several linking challenges with the possibility for grammatical errors. For example, in *Grammar Expert Basic*, students encounter "That man owns_a company" (Bideleux & Mackie, 2007, p. 27), requiring students to link the final /nz/ in owns with the vowel /ʌ/. Dropping the final –s when saying third person verbs is common to English learners (Folse, 2009). However, this is often a pronunciation, rather than grammatical, error stemming from the difficulty of pronouncing blended consonants (see Chapter 10). Clearly, students need guidance and practice with linking the final –s in present tense verbs as well as possessives and plurals.

Core prosodic features are all useful when practicing the simple present. The easiest prosodic feature to hear is the focus word, the most prominent word in each phrase or short sentence. This word sounds longer and louder than the others and changes pitch. Since English speakers exaggerate the strong and weak beats more than speakers of other languages do, students need awareness of these strong beats. In general, the last stressed word of a phrase or sentence receives the strongest stress.

However, as conversations proceed, this focus word often shifts positions. English learners may not intuitively guess the meaning behind the use of focus, much less how prominence shifts as conversations proceed. However, they can build this awareness by listening to short dialogues that illustrate conversational patterns with shifting focus due to new information becoming old information. In this example, the bolded focus words show new information shifting positions.

> A: I want a **DOG**.
>
> B: Don't you **HAVE** a dog?
>
> A: I want a **QUIET** dog. One that doesn't **BARK**.
>
> B: They **ALL** bark. Why not get a **CAT**?
>
> A: **YEAH,** but I'm a**LLER**gic to cats.

Beginning students need listening tasks along with choral practice and physical movement to build awareness of the strong and weak beats of English prosody. Most grammar texts provide CDs with a wealth of listening opportunities. Mendelsohn (1995), in his strategic approach to developing listening skills, underscores the importance of focused listening for one target at a time. After listening several times to clarify the meaning and complete any grammar activities, students could listen, underline the focus words, and then practice the dialogue elongating and raising the pitch on the focus word. They could listen for stressed syllables and circle them. Finally, students could listen for final –s and indicate by checking *yes* or *no* or by showing thumbs up or thumbs down, if they heard it.

In addition to body movement, choral practice, and focused listening as basic strategies for imprinting English prosody, many teachers use songs, poetry, and chants as an invaluable part of their pronunciation repertoire. According to researchers such as Salcedo (2012) and Moradi and Shahrokhi (2014), music helps students internalize English pronunciation rules. Simply put, the brain loves patterns, including musical patterns. It remembers patterned information better than strings of data in the same way that a young child can learn the alphabet through song, but not as a series of 26 letters (Thaut, 2005). Learning songs that echo natural speech patterns, such as folk songs and children's songs, facilitates internalizing both prosody and grammar. For example, the American folk song "Home on the Range" can help students review the simple present and internalize focus, where the song clearly stresses last important word in each chunk. "Oh give me a HOME, where the buffalo ROAM" (Miller, 2007, p. 137).

Listening and speaking improve together. In general, if students can't hear the target structure, they will have difficulty producing it. Moreover, students often struggle to understand streams of spoken English, even after they know the grammar and could easily understand the same sentence when written. Listening to short chunks of speech on the CDs accompanying grammar texts or on authentic TV or YouTube recordings can improve the comprehension of longer speech streams (see Chapter 5). Students benefit enormously from repeated exposure to the same listening text while focusing on different prosodic features.

Integrating Pronunciation and the Simple Past

A beginning grammar course invariably explores the simple past. Teachers often believe the irregular past to be the trickiest aspect of mastering past tenses; however, using regular past tenses in conversation creates pronunciation challenges that can impede communication (see Chapter 12). Unfortunately, when students are taught to add –ed to regular verbs, often little time is spent on the pronunciation rules associated with the change in tense. A casual review of several grammar series reveals that explicit information about how to link –ed to vowel and consonant sounds in the next word is missing. Nonetheless, most past tense verbs occur in the middle of a phrase or sentence, thus requiring linking and often reductions of unstressed words.

Linking can be a difficult, nonetheless crucial, skill for English learners to master. Many students assume that they have to pronounce each sound or syllable clearly, thus producing equal stress patterns that are not characteristic of English speech. They are relieved to learn how to link past tense endings to the next word in a way that sounds more native-like and hence more easily understood. This is reinforced by what they hear fluent speakers say. For instance, *missed him* becomes /**mɪs**tɪm/, dropping the /h/ from *him*. *Watched TV* becomes /wɒtʃtivi/, and the *–ed* ending students are working so hard to master disappears when this phrase is linked. Learning about linking and how the pronunciation of words can change in connected speech improves speech comprehension along with fostering fluent speech.

Linking *–ed* to words starting with consonants is challenging because many students do not blend two or more consonants when speaking their native language. For example, students may struggle with *He asked me* and *[I] started cutting* (Pavlik, 2012, p. 188). These students often drop the *–ed* ending when speaking, even when they know the grammar rule. Thus, what sounds like a grammatical error is likely to be a pronunciation error. When aware of this, teachers can spend more class time reviewing blending consonants.

As with all grammatical forms, listening exercises are essential to teaching the pronunciation of past tense endings. After listening for meaning, teachers can have students listen for past tense endings, eventually highlighting the endings on a transcript. In addition to listening to live or recorded speech models, students develop crucial self-monitoring skills by listening to recordings of their own speech and determining whether they hear the *–ed* ending. Students are often surprised when they think they are saying the past tense, but do not hear it on the recording.

Dictations, another type of listening task, are also an effective way to demonstrate the difference between what learners think they hear and what is actually being said. Teachers can read aloud a list of sentences containing the past tense for students to write that contain linked words, especially those linking /t/ or /d/ or to an unstressed and reduced pronoun, such as *him, her,* or *them,* as in *I wanted them to leave.*

Some educators might shudder at encouraging students to link by eliminating letters or syllables in unstressed words, often "misunderstood as 'lazy' or 'sloppy' speech. However, assimilation is a universal feature of spoken language. In English, it occurs frequently" (Celce-Murcia, Brinton, & Goodwin, 2010, p. 167). In truth, native speakers, even in professional and academic settings, regularly link and reduce words. It does our students a disservice to shield them from this, as they end up having a harder time both comprehending and producing fluent English speech. Linking, and its accompanying reduction of sounds and sometimes syllables, is an essential feature for clear communication and should be taught along with all grammar points practiced in connected speech.

Integrating Pronunciation and Singular and Plural Nouns

Learning to use singular and plural nouns challenges the speaker, adding a final *–s* to regular nouns to blend two or more consonants, as in *friends, beds,* and *cell phones.* These examples show consonant clusters linked to vowels and consonants:

These PINEapples are from **BRAZIL**.

I have FOUR **GLASSES**.

(Schoenberg & Maurer, 2012, p. 8)

Again, linking words challenges students whose native language does not blend two or more consonants. To help negotiate difficult consonant clusters, have students repeat the connected speech starting from the last letter, adding a sound with each pass. With the example *months for*, students would chorally repeat *for*, then *sfor*, then *tsfor*, and finally *montsfor*.

Learning grammar rules about nouns and verbs invariably introduces new vocabulary (see Chapter 1). From the time students learn their first two-syllable word, they need to use word stress. Unfortunately, most students do not know where to place stress in a multisyllabic word or how to lengthen and raise the pitch of the stressed syllable. Nor do they know how to decode the varied stress markings in dictionaries. Dictionary work, listening activities, and keeping a personal glossary can build awareness of word stress. For a beginner activity, teachers can have students choose 10 words from their text to record individually and in short phrases. Teachers then listen and record corrections, asking students to circle the stressed syllable they hear.

When learning singular and plural nouns, beginning students may encounter expressions of measurement. Again, use choral practice to imprint the speech rhythm along with learning the grammar and vocabulary of these short speech units.

a BAG (small clap) of **RICE** (big clap and lean forward)

a BAR of **SOAP**

a BOTTLE of **BEER**

(Azar & Hagen, 2006, p. 150)

Interestingly, the rhythm of common longer words can match the rhythm of short phrases. For example, *converSAtion* matches *Have a **COOK**ie*. Similarly, *fanTAStic* has the same rhythm as *It's **PLAS**tic* and *Let's **FAX** it*. Students enjoy the Echo Game (Miller, 2007), using body movement to practice this connection. Teachers divide the class into two groups: speakers and echoes. The speakers say a multisyllabic word, such as *inviTAtion* while thrusting up both arms on the stressed syllable. The echoes answer with a short sentence matching the word stress pattern, such as *See you **LA**ter*, also raising their arms to show stress.

Integrating Pronunciation and Simple Modal Verbs

Modals are auxiliary, or helping, verbs that add meaning to the main verb. Beginning grammar texts inevitably introduce simple modals. Typically, *Basic English Grammar* covers modals of ability, advice, necessity, request, and suggestion, summarized in a chart (Azar & Hagen, 2006, p. 399). Modals, like all auxiliary verbs, are normally unstressed and reduced. For example, *You should see a doctor* sounds like "You sh'd SEE a **DOC**tor."

A common modal introduced in beginning grammar texts is *can*. Understanding the difference between *can* and *can't* is relatively simple. However, communication often breaks down when these terms are used in conversation, in part because proficient English speakers expect to hear the helping verb *can* reduced to /kən/. If a student pronounces *can* clearly in *I can drive*, it might sound like the negative *can't*. Further complicating things, the pronunciation rules change when *can* and *can't* are pronounced alone as a full verb, as in *We **CAN!*** and *We **CAN'T!***, and neither is reduced.

It is helpful to give students a strategy for advancing communication when being misunderstood. Instead of merely repeating what they just said, speakers can learn how to clarify their message by changing it in some way. For example, suggest that students say *can* or *can't* more strongly, using it as a full verb, instead of as a helping verb. They can say *I **CAN***, lengthening the vowel and raising the pitch, or *I **CAN'T***, lengthening the vowel, raising the pitch, and lightly adding the final *t* sound.

For communicative practice, teachers can instruct listeners to nod affirmatively when they hear a sentence with *can* and shake their heads negatively when they hear *can't*, so speakers can confirm that their message was received. Another activity is the Let's Talk pair work activity, as shown in *Basic English Grammar* (Azar & Hagen, 2014, p. 366). Students ask their partners questions like "Can you ride a motorcycle?" reducing the modal to [c'n]. Students answer using *can* or *can't* in a sentence, as in "i c'n PLAY **TEN**nis" or "i **CAN'T** PLAY TENnis." Listeners hearing *can* write a check. If the listener hears *can't*, the speaker writes an X. Practice reducing *can* helps students learn to reduce other helping verbs and modals.

Integrating Pronunciation and the Present Continuous

According to Folse's (2006) catalogue of common learner errors, students make fewer pronunciation mistakes when uttering sentences containing the present continuous tense than when they use the simple present tenses. Nonetheless, speaking in the present continuous invites an awareness of speech rhythm and the contrast between main verbs and unstressed auxiliary verbs. For example:

The WEAther is **NICE** / at the **MO**ment. / It's NOT **RAIN**ing.

Look at **SUE**. / She's **WEAR**ing / her NEW **HAT**.

(Murphy, 1999, p. 14)

Students need to be aware that if speakers stress the auxiliary and full verbs equally, they unintentionally may sound insistent or agitated (Gilbert, 2008).

Teaching the present continuous can also provide an opportunity to integrate speech groups, or thought groups, into the lessons. Proficient English speakers use their voices to organize speech and make it easier to understand. They say phone numbers, credit card numbers, and addresses in chunks, using stressed numbers followed by pauses to make these easier to follow (see Chapter 5). For example, the phone number 3104502876 would be hard to understand unless said as 31**0** (pause) 45**0** (pause) 287**6** (pause).

Although the sentences in beginning texts tend to be short, students still need to learn how to parse their sentences into chunks to increase their intelligibility, or else "listeners have difficulty understanding, no matter how clearly each word is pronounced" (Grant, 2009, p. 77). Students with a heavy accent can improve their comprehensibility by using more pauses and speech groups, each chunk containing a pitch change on the focus word.

To raise awareness about speech groups, have students listen to the CDs accompanying their grammar books and identify the speech groups by drawing slashes where they hear pauses. To further reinforce the speech rhythm, have students listen again and underline the focus words. Students can also practice speech groups by slashing sentences in their texts into smaller chunks. For example, in *Essential Grammar in Use, Elementary* (Murphy, 1999), "We're staying at the Central Hotel" could become more listener-friendly: "We're staying / at the Central Hotel."

Students can also use a narrative to practice chunking sentences into speech groups, which works well when teaching both the simple past tense and the present continuous. Woodward's (1997) *Fun With Grammar* shows a picture of a busy park scene. Students narrate a story describing the picture using the present continuous. To introduce the idea of chunking, have students write out their narrative and decide where to divide it into speech groups before sharing their story with a partner or small group. Although beginners usually create short sentences, "slowing the rate of speech and combining words into meaningful chunks can improve fluency as well as overall intelligibility" (Levis & Grant, 2003, p. 16).

Integrating Pronunciation and the Simple Future Tense

When studying the future simple tense, students encounter two forms: *will* and *be going to*. Azar and Hagen (2014) kick off the chapter on the simple future with sentences such as "I'm going to eat dinner at home tonight" and "We're going to come to class tomorrow morning." As previously stated, longer sentences like these provide an excellent opportunity to introduce students to core prosodic features. To use *be going to* in a natural, fluent way, students need to be aware that auxiliary verbs are unstressed and often reduced; hence *going to* is often pronounced as *gonna*. Although teachers may balk at teaching students this seemingly sloppy reduction, listening closely to speakers giving formal presentations, academic lectures, and even presidential addresses reveals that *gonna* appears more frequently than its clear counterpart.

Activities prompting students to ask and answer questions about the future invite an introduction to English intonation. English is a melodic language with more high and low notes than most other languages. Both male and female speakers use this variation in melody, an essential part of communicating in English. We use intonation to indicate stressed syllables as well as to reveal subtle shades of meaning, such as sarcasm, surprise, boredom, joy, authority, and uncertainty. Proficient speakers of American English also use intonation to supplement punctuation, such as adjusting the pitch line when asking yes/no questions or ending sentences (see Chapter 3). However, intonation is a notoriously difficult feature to teach. It takes time for students to hear speech melody and to become comfortable with intonation. Listening for pitch changes in speech groups and multisyllabic words is helpful, as is discussing why students may feel uncomfortable with English intonation, which seems more exaggerated than in other languages.

Building awareness that speech has a musical quality is a good starting point. To do this, the teacher might invite students to say sentences in their native languages in front of the class. Then the teacher mirrors the melody and rhythm of each sentence. Students often imagine that the teacher can speak their language just from hearing the intonation. Teachers might also have students speak their first language in front of the class and then discuss how their voices move in pitch.

Another tool for practicing intonation is the kazoo, a toy that students hum into.

> Second language learners do not hear intonation very well. When they listen to speech, they are powerfully distracted from paying attention to pitch changes because they are struggling to understand sounds, vocabulary, and grammar. A kazoo is an excellent tool for helping students focus on pitch patterns. (Gilbert, 2008, p. 35)

After students have listened to questions with the simple future, have them hum into their kazoos, paying attention to the intonation. Learning to use enough melody is particularly important because English speech with too little melody not only is difficult to understand but also may send unintended messages. For instance, a student who does not drop the pitch enough at the ends of sentences may unintentionally sound unsure or lacking in confidence.

Integrating Pronunciation and Comparatives and Superlatives

When students learn to use comparative and superlative structures, this invites practice of core pronunciation features, especially syllable count and word stress. For instance, *Essential Grammar in Use* (Murphy, 1999) contains a familiar chart instructing students to add *-er* to one-syllable nouns and to use *more than* for long words.

Among the core features, focus, or prominence, has been highlighted several times in this chapter because of its importance. English speakers use focus to highlight important information, and listeners use this to process meaning. However, proficient English speakers also shift the focus as conversations proceed in order to draw attention to new information and show contrast. For example, *Fun With Grammar* (Woodward, 1997) contains cards with two items, such as *Grammar book* and *Writing book*, and an adjective, such as *easy*, and students are supposed to make comparative sentences, as in Our **GRA**mmar book is easy / but our **WRI**ting book is easier. Familiarity with focus can help students contrast two things when they practice comparatives.

For a more advanced activity, have students write short dialogues for the class comparing two things and underline the focus words. They can present the dialogues from this script or from memory. For feedback, students listen to or watch a recording of their talk to self-correct, or the instructor marks corrections on the script. Over time, through listening and speaking practice and exposure, learners develop an intuitive use of focus in English conversation.

Conclusion

Preparing a good beginning grammar lesson plan can be a juggling act. Teachers are constrained by an overfilled curriculum and the pressure to meet student needs. Though most educators acknowledge the need to incorporate pronunciation into their classes, the challenge of choosing what to teach and how to fit this into existing materials can seem overwhelming. We believe the answer lies in the prosody package, which can be integrated into existing grammar lessons without creating a whole new set of materials. In fact, teaching this is as easy as 1, 2, 3!

1. Be prepared. Listen for these high-priority features everywhere you hear English—on TV, in movies, and in conversations. As teachers and proficient English speakers, you already know these features and use them every time you speak. However, you may not have named them or identified them as crucial to clear communication. Along with your students, do a lot of listening. You will hear the prosodic features of spoken English more clearly when you learn to listen beyond the meaning of the words and tune in to the music of the phrase.

2. Point out these key features and practice them with students as you teach grammar, introduce new vocabulary, and create conversations.

3. Use focused listening, body movement, and choral practice to reinforce your lessons.

By teaching with these strategies in mind, it becomes easier to seamlessly integrate pronunciation practice into the ESL and EFL curricula.

Resources

Gilbert, J. (2008). *Teaching pronunciation: Using the prosody pyramid*. Cambridge, England: Cambridge University Press.

Gilbert, J. (2102). *Clear speech*. Cambridge, England: Cambridge University Press.

Grant, L. (2006). *Well said intro: Pronunciation for clear communication*. Boston, MA: Heinle.

Grant, L. (2009). *Well said: Pronunciation for clear communication* (3rd ed.). Boston, MA: Heinle.

Hancock, M. (1996). *Pronunciation games*. Cambridge, England: Cambridge University Press.

Meyers, C., & Holt, S. (2001). *Pronunciation teacher training*. Burnsville, MN: Aspen Productions.

Miller, S. (2007). *Targeting pronunciation: Communicating clearly in English*. Independence, KY: Cengage.

Noll, M. (2007). *American accent skills, book 1: Intonation, reductions and word connections*. Oakland, CA: Ameritalk Press.

References

Azar, B., & Hagen, S. (2014). *Basic English grammar* (4th ed.). White Plains, NY: Pearson Education.

Bideleux, S., & Mackie, G. (2007). *Grammar expert, basic*. Boston, MA: Thompson Heinle.

Celce-Murcia, M., Brinton, D. M., & Goodwin, J. M. (2010). *Teaching pronunciation: A reference for teachers of English to speakers of other languages*. New York, NY: Cambridge University Press.

Derwing, T. M., & Rossiter, M. J. (2003). The effects of pronunciation instruction on the accuracy, fluency and complexity of L2 accented speech. *Applied Language Learning, 13*, 1–18.

Folse, K. (2006). *The art of teaching speaking*. Ann Arbor: University of Michigan Press.

Folse, K. (2009). *Keys to teaching grammar to English language learners*. Ann Arbor: University of Michigan Press.

Gilbert, J. (2001). Six pronunciation priorities for the beginning student. *CATESOL Journal, 13*, 173–182.

Gilbert, J. (2008). *Teaching pronunciation: Using the prosody pyramid*. Cambridge, England: Cambridge University Press.

Grant, L. (2009). *Well said: Pronunciation for clear communication* (3rd ed.). Boston, MA: Heinle.

Kjellin, O. (1999). Accent addition: Prosody and perception facilitates second language learning. In O. Fujimura, B. D. Joseph, & B. Palek (Eds.), *Proceedings of LP'98 Linguistics and Phonetics Conference: Vol. 2* (pp. 373–398). Columbus, OH: Karolinum Press.

Levis, J. M., & Grant, L. (2003). Integrating pronunciation into ESL/EFL classrooms. *TESOL Journal, 12*(2), 13–19.

Mendelsohn, D. (1994). *Learning to listen: A strategy-based approach for the second language learner*. San Diego, CA: Dominie Press.

Meyers, C., & Holt, S. (2001). *Pronunciation for success*. Burnsville, MN: Aspen Productions.

Miller, S. (2007). *Targeting pronunciation: Communicating clearly in English*. Independence, KY: Cengage.

Moradi, F., & Shahrokhi, M. (2014). The effect of listening to music on Iranian children's segmental and suprasegmental pronunciation. *English Language Teaching, 7*(6), 128–142.

Murphy, R. (1999). *Essential grammar in use, elementary*. Cambridge, England: Cambridge University Press.

Pavlik, C. (2012). *Grammar sense 1* (2nd ed.). Oxford, England: Oxford University Press.

Salcedo, C. S. (2010). The effects of songs in the foreign language classroom on text recall, delayed text recall and involuntary mental rehearsal. *Journal of College Teaching and Learning, 7*(6), 19–30.

Schoenburg, I. E., & Maurer, J. (2012). *Focus on grammar 1, workbook* (3rd ed.). White Plains, NY: Pearson Education.

Thaut, M. H. (2005). *Rhythm, music, and the brain: Scientific foundations and clinical applications*. London, England: Taylor & Francis.

Woodward, S. W. (1997). *Fun with grammar*. Upper Saddle River, NJ: Prentice Hall Regents.

CHAPTER 8

The Integration of Pronunciation and Intermediate Grammar Instruction

Monika Floyd

Today's integrated and contextualized approach to grammar teaching is based on the insight that content and meaning are of paramount importance when it comes to learning how to communicate in a foreign language (Celce-Murcia, 2002; Pennington, 2002). A learner's motivation is driven by his or her curiosity to deconstruct and construct meaning that finds its expression in the ubiquitous questions "What does this mean?" and "How can I say this?" Students, therefore, need to develop a multifaceted array of knowledge in order to develop communicative competence, including the skills to understand and be understood in speaking and writing the new language.

When acquiring a new language, all of these skills are equally important and go hand in hand. Sometimes the teacher will need to focus more on lexical items, morphology, and syntactic structures; at other times the teacher will emphasize important pronunciation rules.

This chapter is situated at the intersection of intermediate grammar structures and their pronunciation. In order to highlight the connections between the two, it presents pronunciation activities that enhance the teaching of intermediate grammar structures in meaningful contexts.

Questions

There are basically three types of grammatical questions that are covered in the intermediate ESL classroom: *wh–* questions, yes/no questions, and tag questions. Whereas the different grammatical structures are dealt with in great detail in common textbooks, the differences in pronunciation are usually neglected. For students, however, it is very helpful to understand that there are significant differences in the intonation of the various question types. Intonation is commonly described as the pitch of the voice, which can either rise and become higher or sharper or fall to a lower pitch level. These are called *rising* and *falling intonation*, respectively. This section describes the intonation rules for the different types of questions.

Wh– questions start with an interrogative (e.g., *who, where, when, what, why, how*), and the speaker's voice most often should go down at the end of the question. One of the most prominent examples is the question "What's this?" which clearly demands a falling pitch on the last word of the question.

Yes/no questions usually start with an auxiliary (e.g., *is, are, was, were, do, does, did*). These types of questions usually carry an up-rise intonation in North American English. On the last content word of the question, the pitch tends to go down slightly on the stressed syllable and then up, as in "Do you have a question?" (↘↗).

The tag question is a two-part structure: a statement with an attached short question, the tag. There are two types. The first type is the same-polarity tag question, in which the statement and the tag are positive, as in "You get it, do you?" The second type is the opposite-polarity tag question, with the verb in the statement and the verb in the tag of opposite value, as in "This isn't difficult, is it?" The intonation in a tag question can be either rising or falling. Here are some rules of thumb: In the same-polarity tag question, the intonation in North American English usually rises, as in "We will be on time, will we?" (↘↗). In the opposite-polarity tag question, the intonation can be either rising or falling, depending on the context. If the speaker seeks information, the intonation is rising, as in "You understand what I mean, don't you?" (↘↗). However, if the speaker assumes that the listener will agree with the statement, the intonation is falling, as in "That was easy, wasn't it?" (↗↘).

Integrated Intonation Practice

Interviews, surveys, dialogues, and excerpts of plays are texts that are usually rich in questions and can serve as excellent springboards for pronunciation practice. Students will better understand and remember intonation differences if they are visible. Therefore it is recommended to adapt a system that shows rising and falling intonation. This could be expressed by adding arrows over the text or drawing lines under or over the text, indicating the direction of the voice.

A good way for students to get a feel for different intonation patterns is via listening activities. While listening to a speaker, students read the spoken text and at the same time mark the prominent word(s), which they can then compare with a partner after the exercise. To create awareness of different intonation patterns, students could analyze a textbook text, an interview, or a dialogue and determine the question type. After that they would add arrows or lines indicating the required intonation. In a second step, they could read the text aloud in pairs or record themselves (for more activities, see Chapter 3).

Here are some additional practice ideas:

- Emulating a speaker's intonation is a great opportunity to learn correct intonation. This could be done in class or individually using recorded audio or video.

- Jazz chants (Graham, 1978) help students practice question patterns. Listening to and repeating those humorous songs can be a nice 5-minute activity at the beginning as an icebreaker or at the end of a lesson.

- Design questionnaires and interview a partner. Possible topics include family or vacation plans.

- Play the game Jeopardy and prepare answers for which students have to come up with the right question.

- Play the game Guess Who? Ask one student to pretend to be a famous person, and have the other students find out who she or he is by asking yes/no questions. As with all the above-mentioned activities, it is important that the teacher carefully monitors and gives feedback on students' pronunciation to ensure they are using the appropriate pronunciation.

Adjectives and Adverbs

The correct pronunciation of English adjectives and adverbs requires a good understanding of the importance of stress in words. In general, there is only one stressed syllable in each word. But there can be many syllables in one word. Therefore it is important for students to be able to recognize syllables.

Generally put, a syllable is a letter or a combination of letters that are pronounced together. There are several ways to teach this concept; a common way is to have students clap the beat of the syllables. Another option is to have students feel the beats. By placing a hand under the jaw and pronouncing a word, they will feel how the jaw taps the hand for each syllable. A stressed syllable is marked by the following features: It is pronounced louder, longer, and higher in pitch. In addition, it is pronounced more clearly, and if you carefully look at the speaker's facial expression, you can see larger facial movements around the jaw and lips.

Adjectives

The rules for short adjectives are fairly straightforward: There is no problem with stress in one-syllable words like *hot, cold, warm, short, long, nice, big,* and *tall.* In two-syllable adjectives the stress usually falls on the root of the word, which can be in the first or second syllable. Research has shown that the most frequently used two-syllable adjectives are predominantly stressed on the first syllable (Seattle Learning Academy,

2008–2011). Here are some examples of adjectives that are stressed on the first sylla-
ble: **hap**py, **ea**sy, **hun**gry, **fa**mous, **plea**sant, **cau**tious, **help**ful, **care**ful, **use**less, **flaw**less.
If the root is in the second syllable, the second syllable is stressed: com**plete**, a**live**,
in**tense**, sur**real**, ex**treme**, pre**cise**.

As adjectives become more complex, so do the rules that govern how they are
stressed. Table 1 presents an overview of a few rules pertaining to the stress in words
that end in a particular suffix. (See Chapters 1 and 2 for more information related
to word forms.)

Adverbs

The modifier of a verb in a sentence is called an adverb. Many adverbs end in –*ly* (e.g.,
clearly, *nicely*, *sweetly*). However, there are also adverbs, especially high-frequency
adverbs, that do not carry an –*ly* ending (e.g., *often*, *always*, *seldom*, *never*, *sometimes*).
The pronunciation rule for two-syllable adverbs is similar to that for adjectives. The
syllable that carries the root is stressed (e.g., **neat**ly, **warm**ly, **poor**ly, **just**ly, **safe**ly,
per**haps**, in**deed**, un**less**). As you can clearly see, the majority of these adverbs carry
the stress on the first syllable.

Numerals present another challenge for students in terms of pronunciation.
Expressing numbers, especially teens and tens, as in thir**teen** and **thir**ty, four**teen** and
forty, fif**teen** and **fif**ty, proves to be difficult for many students of English. In general,
the rule states that the tens are stressed on the first syllable and the teens are stressed
on the second, the –*teen* syllable. However, in spoken discourse the –*teen* syllable is
often not very pronounced, and the difference is very difficult for a nonnative speaker
to discern. In addition, the /t/ sound in numbers like *thir*ty, *for*ty, and *eighty* is voiced
and sounds like /d/ in North American English (see Chapter 1).

Integrated Pronunciation Practice

Raising students' awareness of word stress helps them become more confident in
their understanding of the sound structure of words and of the tendencies and patterns of word stress. Guiding questions could be: How many syllables are in this
word? Which syllable is stressed? How can you tell which syllable should be stressed?
Which syllable appears to be unstressed and why? Can you provide a word with a
similar syllable or stress pattern?

When introducing a new vocabulary word, students need to know not only its
part of speech and its meaning but also which syllable is stressed. They should adopt
a system that helps them remember the pronunciation of the word. Some students
may be versed in the International Phonetic Alphabet; others may need to resort to
an accent or a line on the stressed syllable or even to a completely different denotation system, such as small and big circles, or thin and fat lines symbolizing the

Table 1 Stress and Suffixes

SUFFIX	WHERE STRESS IS CARRIED
Adjectives that end in *-ic/-tic* • spe**cif**ic • proble**ma**tic • ec**sta**tic • opti**mis**tic	on the syllable that precedes the suffix
Adjectives that end in *-ical/-tical* • eco**nom**ical • I**den**tical • theo**ret**ical • **vert**ical	on the syllable immediately before the suffix
Adjectives that end in *-ial/-ual* • arti**fi**cial • fi**nan**cial • un**u**sual • **mu**tual	on the syllable that precedes the suffix
Adjectives that end in *-ient* • ef**fic**ient • **an**cient • suf**fic**ient • pro**fic**ient	on the syllable preceding the suffix
Adjectives that end in *-cious/-tious* • am**bit**ious • de**li**cious • su**spi**cious • **cau**tious	on the syllable preceding the suffix
Adjectives that end in *-ible* • **e**dible • in**vin**cible • im**pos**sible • **fle**xible	right before the suffix

pattern (e.g., O o o for *wonderful*). Many visual learners will appreciate being able to see a stress pattern. You could therefore make it a routine to always mark the stress of new vocabulary clearly on the board or in your handouts.

Auditory and tactile learners will respond to a multimodal presentation of stress in words. Clapping out patterns—soft claps for unstressed and loud claps for stressed syllables—is one way to highlight word stress. Students could also use rubber bands that: To feel and visualize word stress, students pull both sides of a rubber band to the end to demonstrate the stressed syllable. If you have a variety of paper clips on hand, students could connect short paper clips to unstressed syllables and long paper clips to stressed syllables. This activity can also be done with Cuisenaire rods, or color-coded blocks, to help visualize stress patterns. Students must also be aware of the how dictionaries normally mark stress: with a mark before the stressed syllable (e.g., 'apple). By knowing this, students will be able to check word stress independently.

Pronouns and Reflexive Pronouns

Personal pronouns that grammatically substitute a noun or a noun phrase are monosyllabic words that in spoken discourse frequently are considered function or structure words, as they provide little or no new detail. The pronunciation of function words is connected to the concept of reduction or de-emphasis of speech, which to many learners of ESL is an unknown source and needs to be taught (see Chapter 5).

Function Words Versus Content Words

In spoken discourse, we differentiate two categories of words: content and function. Content words carry new information; very often are nouns and verbs; and are pronounced louder, longer, and higher in pitch in contrast to function words. Function words are less important for the meaning and usually comprise pronouns, prepositions, conjunctions, auxiliary verbs, determiners, modals, and quantifiers. It is important for students to understand that English speakers expect some words to be stressed more than other words and that de-emphasis does not mean that the speaker is lazy or sloppy in terms of articulation. As Gilbert (2005) stated, "the English learner's main difficulty with focus is not learning how to emphasize the focus word, but learning how to de-emphasize the other words" (p. 31).

This is all the more true in connected discourse, when unstressed pronouns become even further reduced through the omission of the first consonant sound; for example, there is often a missing h in constructions like *kiss him, get her,* and *did he.* It often seems to be the case that when students study grammar items, such as pronouns, they tend to focus more on the correct word form and less on the correct pronunciation. Teachers, however, need to be aware of this tendency and include practices that make students pay attention to pronunciation rules and mirror real-world discourses as much as possible. For example, the teaching of reflexive pronouns should focus not only on the grammatical form but also on the rule that stress in reflexive pronouns is put on the second syllable *–self* or *–selves* (e.g., my**self**, your**self**, them**selves**, our**selves**).

Integrated Pronunciation Practice

The concept of reduction and de-emphasis can be demonstrated by having students simultaneously listen to and view a written text. They should be able to determine that content words are stressed and function words usually don't carry stress. To visualize this rule, students could circle content words or cross out non-stressed function words in a coherent text. Those annotations in turn could be used for independent reading examples.

To visualize silent letters as the initial /h/ sound in many pronouns, instructors could use the folded sentence technique, as Gilbert (2005) explained in her *Teacher's Resource Book* (p. 34). For that reason, an example sentence, such as *He knows himself*, would be printed on a paper strip and folded so that the omission of the initial /h/ sound would be clearly visible as /*knowsimself*/. Such hands-on pronunciation exercises make the concept of reduction a multimodal experience, which serves kinesthetic students especially well.

Articles

There are two types of articles in English: the definite article *the* and the indefinite article *a* or *an*.

The Definite Article The

Pronunciation of the initial sound /ðə/ in *the* frequently poses a challenge, and students become very creative in substituting *th* with a range of *s* or *f* sounds and *d* sounds. The correct pronunciation, however, is important and instruction should start with an explanation of the sound production. The tip of the tongue is most important in the formation of this sound. It should be placed behind the top front teeth while pushing air between the tip of the tongue and the top front teeth. Some students may find it easier to place the tip of the tongue between the top and bottom front teeth. Demonstrating and modeling this sound is definitely recommended, especially by using graphics of the mouth that indicate the position of the tongue (see Figure 1).

Another helpful tool is a handheld mirror, which allows students to view the correct position of their own tongue. Recording students' pronunciation may also help them become aware of their own pronunciation difficulties. There are several

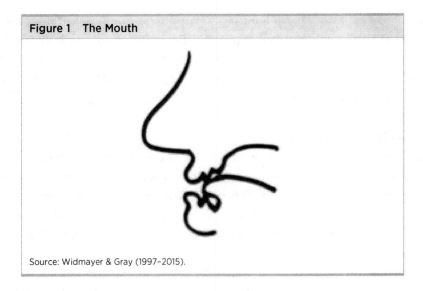

Figure 1   The Mouth

Source: Widmayer & Gray (1997–2015).

websites and apps that students can consult (e.g., Sounds of Speech, hosted by the University of Iowa, http://soundsofspeech.uiowa.edu).

There are two ways to pronounce *the* in a phrase or sentence. Most frequently you hear the article pronounced with the schwa, a very reduced vowel sound. However, the article is alternatively pronounced /ði/ (*thee*) when it precedes a vowel sound (e.g., *the apple, the ear, the uncle*). The other occasion when you hear the article pronounced as /ði/ (*thee*) is when the speaker puts extra emphasis or stress on the following noun (e.g., *I like all Harry Potter books, but this is THE book (as in the most important book) that everyone should read*). What sounds overly emphasized is the expression of excitement (see Chapters 5 and 6 for more information about prominence).

The Indefinite Articles A *and* An

The use of *a* or *an* depends on the initial sound (not the initial letter) of the following word: If it is a vowel sound, then the use of *an* is obligatory (e.g., *an apple, an ear, an idea, an organ, an uncle, an MP3 player*). If the initial sound, however, is not a vowel, *a* suffices (e.g., *a university, a uniform, a European city*).

There are some tricky cases involving the /h/ sound. If it is pronounced, like in the word *hotel*, it is correct to say *a hotel*. This is different when the sound is silent or not pronounced, as in *an hour, an honor*, and *an herb*, although there are exceptions depending on accents and dialects. Likewise, the letter *x* can present problems for students; in words like *x-ray*, the initial sound is the vowel sound /ɛ/ and should be preceded by *an*, while in words like *xylophone*, it sounds like /z/, so it should be preceded by *a*.

Integrated Pronunciation Practice

The concept of reduction and de-emphasis can be demonstrated by listening activities that have students simultaneously listen to and view a written text. For this exercise, the teacher selects an appropriate text and has students first listen to it for content. After that, students are presented with a written version of the listening text and asked to listen to the text again, this time with a pencil in hand so that they can underline stressed words. A discussion of the results should emphasize that, in general, content words carry stress. In order to demonstrate the reduced pronunciation of articles, the exercise should be continued with another listening-while-reading task, this time asking students to cross out non-stressed articles in the text. By reviewing the answers, students will visually recognize how little stress articles receive and how important the concept of de-emphasis is in spoken discourse.

These types of listening-while-reading activities literally highlight the specific melody and prosody of English and can be conducted on all levels. For beginners the texts can be shorter; for intermediate and more advanced students, there are more complex texts in textbooks or on the Internet. Great examples are speeches that students can listen to while reading and marking stress. Classic examples are Martin Luther King's "I Have a Dream" speech (1963), Kevin Rudd's "The Stolen Generation" speech (2008), and some of Barack Obama's speeches, with the "A More Perfect Union" speech (2008) the best known. In addition, intermediate and advanced students can benefit from analyzing TED talks, which are available as videos with transcripts, translations, and additional information on the TED website (www.ted.com).

Songs are also popular with many students and could be turned into pronunciation activities. In order to focus on the de-emphasis of articles, songs could be presented as a cloze activity: Delete all articles and have students fill in the gaps while listening to the song. Afterward, check students' listening comprehension by repeating the correct version or singing the song.

Phrasal Verbs

Phrasal verbs consist of a verb and one or more particles that together form a semantic unit. At first glance, the particles look like prepositions; however, phrasal verbs, in fact, function neither as prepositions nor as adverbs, for example: "When John runs *out on* Maria and runs *off with* another woman, Maria tracks him *down* to do him *in*" (Kohnhorst, 2003, p. III).

Phrasal verbs present special challenges regarding the proper placement of stress: either on the verb or on the particle following the verb (see Chapter 1). An example of a phrasal verb that places the stress on the verb and leaves the particle unstressed is *look at* (e.g., *I **looked** at the bill and fainted*). Other phrasal verbs have two stresses:

stronger stress on the particle and less pronounced stress on the verb. Examples of such phrasal verbs include *take **off*** (e.g., *His flight must **take off** on time for him to make his connection to the next flight*), *blow **over*** (e.g., *We should just keep quiet until the scandal **blows over***), and *come **to*** (e.g., *After the accident, he was in a coma for several months before he finally **came to***). When a preposition follows a phrasal-verb particle, that preposition remains unstressed and the phrasal-verb particle retains its stress (e.g., *He had to **make up** for it*; for more examples, see Underhill, 2005).

Integrated Pronunciation Practice

To help students become aware of the complexity of phrasal verb stress patterns, start by having them compare and contrast the stress and intonation placed on phrasal verbs and on compound nouns.

Phrasal Verbs	Compound Nouns
work *out*	*work*out
drop *out*	*drop*out
print *out*	*print*out
cover *up*	*cover*-up
run *off*	*run*off
tear *off*	*tear*-off

(Miller, 2006, p. 65)

In addition, English learners can benefit from activities that raise awareness and highlight the stress patterns of phrasal verbs in context. This can be done with the help of poems and songs that contain a variety of phrasal verbs (e.g., "Hung Up" by Madonna, "Sk8ter Boy" by Avril Lavigne, "Breakaway" by Kelly Clarkson). These lyrics could be used to produce a gap-fill activity by eliminating some phrasal verbs. When students listen to the songs, they have to focus on the phrasal verbs by completing the gaps with the missing words. As a follow-up activity, students could engage in a karaoke performance and sing the song, emulating the artist.

As another communicative activity with a focus on specific phrasal verbs, have students draw flashcards with phrasal verbs from a hat and create funny stories that they can read out loud or talk about while being carefully monitored for appropriate pronunciation (cf. Miller, 2006, p. 67).

Conclusion

The isolated teaching of form, meaning, and usage of syntactic structures has long been at the forefront. Today, however, in a tightly connected, more globalized world with many variants of English, clear expressiveness is becoming increasingly important. Teaching should therefore focus on students' intelligibility and comprehensibility in ways that allow for clear communication. As shown in a variety of examples, this can be accomplished in the early stages of the foreign language acquisition process when the instruction of syntactic structures and pronunciation go hand in hand, enrich each other, and thereby lead to a comprehensive command of English as a foreign language.

References

Celce-Murcia, M. (2002). Why it makes sense to teach grammar in context and through discourse. In E. Hinkel & S. Fotos (Eds.), *New perspectives on grammar teaching in second language classrooms* (pp. 119–133). New York, NY: Routledge.

Gilbert, J. (2005). *Clear speech: Pronunciation and listening comprehension in North American English, teacher's resource book* (3rd ed.). New York, NY: Cambridge University Press.

Graham, C. (1978). *Jazz chants*. New York, NY: Oxford University Press.

Kohnhorst, K. (2003). *A phrasal verb affair*. Brattleboro, VT: Pro Lingua Associates.

Miller, S. (2006). *Targeting pronunciation: Communicating clearly in English*. Boston, MA: Houghton Mifflin.

Pennington, M. (2002). Grammar and communication: New directions in theory and practice. In E. Hinkel & S. Fotos (Eds.), *New perspectives on grammar teaching in second language classrooms* (pp. 77–98). New York, NY: Routledge.

Seattle Learning Academy. (2008–2011). *2-syllable word stress*. Retrieved from http://www.pronuncian.com/Podcast/Default.aspx?Episode=130

Underhill, A. (2005). Pronunciation and phrasal verbs. *MED Magazine, 34*. Retrieved from http://www.macmillandictionaries.com/resources/med-magazine/

Widmayer, S., & Gray, H. (1997–2015). *Sounds of English*. Retrieved from http://www.soundsofenglish.org/pronunciation/th.html

CHAPTER 9

Integrating Pronunciation With Advanced Grammar

Wayne Rimmer

Priorities and Opportunities

Grammar has traditionally been the cornerstone of the English language teaching curriculum. Even in methodologies that are less explicitly form-focused, such as the communicative approach, teachers and learners appreciate the input of grammatical items and opportunities to practise them. Nowhere is this more evident than in four-skill textbooks, which for all their claims for distinctiveness and originality are largely organised around grammatical content that is predictable in its choice and selection of items (cf. the survey by Tomlinson & Masuhara, 2013). The pervasiveness and influence of textbooks is such that they basically consist of the syllabus for most courses, so, wittingly or unwittingly, the vast majority of teachers are following a grammar syllabus (Rimmer, 2013).

This means that pronunciation typically plays a very secondary role to grammar. Less time is allocated to pronunciation teaching (Marks, 2014), especially since the advent of the communicative approach (Levis, 2005), and the points selected usually complement the grammar (Rimmer, 2014); for example, the past simple provides an opportunity to highlight the extra syllable on some *-ed* endings (*loot/ed* vs. *looked*). In a textbook-based lesson, which to reiterate is the norm, the pronunciation component is the most minor and optional in that leaving out the grammar would destroy the coherence and point of the lesson, whereas skipping the pronunciation box would hardly register.

Grammar is thus the dominant factor in virtually any programme. Certainly, there is far more consensus over the inclusion and sequencing of grammatical items than there could be in an equivalent pronunciation syllabus.

Try this little experiment: Take the following complex sentences and put them in the order that you would teach them:

If I had been late again, I would have been in trouble.

If it rains, you get wet.

If I see Sara, I'll tell her.

If I had more time, I'd study French.

Chances are that you would come up with the following:

If it rains, you get wet.

If I see Sara, I'll tell her.

If I had more time, I'd study French.

If I had been late again, I would have been in trouble.

This is easy because you recognise the familiar sequence of conditional sentences, conveniently numbered 0–3 in textbooks. The fact that this neat picture is far from representative of patterns incorporating an *if* clause (cf. Tilbury, 2008) seems not to deter us in our anxiety to impose order on language.

Now try to do the same thing with some consonant sounds. Put these in the order that you would teach them: *g, l, m, n, s*. This is immediately more difficult. Most teachers would not know where to start because they have never seen this done in the materials they use. One principle might be frequency, the assumption being that, as with vocabulary, we should teach the more common items first. This would give us *n, s, l, m, g* according to the frequency statistics in Cruttenden (2014). However, frequency doesn't really work with pronunciation because, unlike grammar and vocabulary, we need everything at once to say even the most basic utterances. The familiar refrain of grading your language is not applicable to pronunciation because all the segmental and suprasegmental features are distributed, albeit unevenly, across speech right at the elementary levels (Marks & Bowen, 2012).

A more selective strategy such as building a pronunciation syllabus around items relevant and problematic for a particular group of learners is similarly hard to implement. Proponents of English as a lingua franca (ELF)—Jenkins (2000) is the seminal work—argue that this is systematic and efficient: There is no point wasting time on sounds such as ð, which have minimal communicative load; ð occurs in several unaccented functional words like *the* and *that* or on features that are fairly language universal, like a rising tone for questions. However, this falls apart if you teach the kind of multilingual groups familiar in an ESL context because learners' needs and problems will be different. Also, because ELF is a medium of communication, not a variety like, say, Nigerian English (Walker, 2010), it cannot be delineated and described in the same way as, say, general American and there are no teaching materials for it. This would create a lot of pressure for teachers to design their own materials and strategies, an unrealistic scenario.

Rather than rejecting the grammar syllabus and trying to substitute something more pronunciation-informed, it is sensible to accept the status quo and look for opportunities to emphasise the link between the grammar and pronunciation, an integrated approach. Learners will pay more attention to the pronunciation if it is central to the core material, the grammar, not marginal. In addition, the teacher can stay with the textbook without the need to completely rethink the lesson and introduce supplementary material. Grammar makes sense to teachers; very rarely do they need to justify teaching it. Pronunciation can make sense too if it has a clear connection to the target language.

In a chapter dealing with advanced grammar, there is the added complication that what we think of as grammar tails off at the higher levels of achievement. For another experiment, write down what new grammar you would expect to see in a textbook for advanced learners. That wasn't easy, was it? For example, it is unlikely your list includes new tenses. All those complex blends of verb aspect and tense, like the past perfect continuous, have been covered at lower levels. The new grammar that is represented in textbooks seems to be rather tangential, like inversion after negative adverbials (*Seldom have I seen . . .*) or the mandatory subjunctive (*I insist he come to the meeting*). The grammar syllabus peters out into consolidation of earlier material and points that are arguably as much lexical, such as verb patterns (e.g., *deny + that/ –ing, urge* + object + *to* infinitive). A survey of advanced-level course books (Rimmer, 2004) confirms this.

The problem, more for textbook writers than learners, is that grammar is essentially a fixed and finite system compared to vocabulary, which is for all learning purposes infinite in size and mutable, with words coming in and disappearing. Accordingly, advanced textbooks concentrate on vocabulary and the grammar tends to be remedial work. This seemingly creates a void for integrating pronunciation into grammar at higher levels unless the learners can tolerate a lot of repetition.

However, the story of grammar does not stop when learners are advanced. First, there is accuracy as learners will still make mistakes, especially when attempting complex structures. This means that grammar revision is definitely worthwhile, and adding a pronunciation element can provide variety and extension. Second, and more pertinent, is that grammar needs a discourse perspective to maintain its relevance. Grammar as discourse is less concerned with forming individual constructions and instead involves learners exploring and deploying the language options that make grammar effective and striking in a specific context of use (the work of Larsen-Freeman, 2003, is critical to this argument). The treatment of pronunciation needs to adopt the same discourse framework so that the successful selection and combination of grammatical features is accentuated by the phonology. It could hardly be otherwise because the most proficient use of grammar would be completely wasted if the utterance was unintelligible and mostly wasted if the phonological and grammatical choices were at odds.

To give an example of a discourse approach to grammar and consequently pronunciation, consider the use of parentheticals, material that is an aside so to speak because it does not fit into the sentence structure. The following example is from the transcript of an interview with Edward Snowden.

> They not only share information, <u>the reporting of results from intelligence,</u> but they actually share the tools and the infrastructure they work together against joint targets in services and there's a lot of danger in this [emphasis added]. (Accessible from www.ndr.de/nachrichten/netzwelt/snowden277.html)

The section in commas, *the reporting of results from intelligence,* is parenthetical, here a noun phrase in apposition to *information.* Grammatically, two noun phrases next to each other, the first a single word, the second fuller with a noun + two prepositional phrases, is an efficient way of packaging the material. The speaker chooses parenthesis to make the argument tighter. In terms of pronunciation, the parenthetical material would be marked off by being in a lower key, flagging that this is an addendum to the main message, and bounded by a pause. In combination, the grammar and pronunciation choices, apposition and pitch/pausing, build up Snowden's sophistry.

Learners can be attuned to discourse grammar and the pronunciation interface by noticing the phenomena and reproducing them in communicative environments. The following section shows how this can be done for three illustrative advanced-level grammatical features by means of activities that are relatively easy to set up and include the textbook as the unifying principle in the curriculum. This is no template for integrating grammar and pronunciation; at higher levels of performance it is hardly possible to predict or condition the language needed and the way it can be exploited. To illustrate, Rimmer (in press) presents a discussion activity encouraging learners to use abstract nouns with finite complement clauses. Learners' attention is drawn to how there is a rise at the end of the first clause/thought group and then a fall on completion: *The thing is* (rise) // *that it's difficult to choose* (fall). However, learners could use alternative constructions to make their point: *It's difficult to choose* is two clauses but one thought group and one pitch movement. Also, in the target language, it is perfectly possible to conceive of a fall rather than a rise on the first thought group. Context is everything, and positing a one-to-one correspondence between a communicative event and a specific construction is as erroneous as aligning emotional state to tone choice, for example, surprise and rise-fall (cf. Cauldwell, 2013). Instead, the following section orientates teachers towards the richness of the grammatical and phonological systems and provides examples of how work on one can contain and complement work on the other.

Classroom Applications

Sentence Structure and Thought Groups

Listening is a difficult skill for many learners because the stream of speech comes at them all in a rush. The written word, in contrast, is neatly chunked and divided up by punctuation, the most obvious being the space between words. Speech may come across as one continuous jumble, but there are breaks, otherwise we wouldn't be able to breathe and speak at the same time. The thought group, or tone unit, is the basic unit of speech before a boundary and this corresponds to the phrase or clause in grammar. Thus, the following written sentence would typically be spoken in two thought groups.

> *On the whole, // I'm pretty pleased with the results.*

The first thought group is a phrase, headed by a preposition, and the second is a clause, centred around a verb. A thought group tends to be separated by a pause, a lengthening at the end, and a change in tone. Getting the thought groups wrong is as bad as getting the grammar wrong in terms of obscuring meaning (see Gilbert, 2014, for more detail), so practice in identifying and pronouncing thought groups is essential. In grammatical parlance this is called *parsing*, putting units into syntactical categories, and it is an equivalent process to forming thought groups. At an advanced level, there should be a high degree of automaticity in locating thought groups and the following activity, shadowing, promotes this.

Shadowing involves learners marking up a recording script for thought groups and then approximating their pronunciation to the recording (for more information on thought groups, see Chapters 5, 11, and 12). The script should be one familiar to the learners so that they don't have to waste a lot of cognitive effort in working out the meaning. A piece from a textbook listening is ideal because learners will already have encountered it and the recording script will be available in full. Transcribing speech from other sources is not practical because a lot of work is involved to get a decent-length text.

The following steps are recommended:

1. Choose a recording just a little below learners' competence.

2. Play the recording and use the usual listening comprehension strategies to make sure learners understand it.

3. Select a portion—two or three paragraphs maximum—for students to mark into thought groups. There is no need to transcribe the section; it will be enough to mark off the thought groups with slashes.

4. Learners listen to the section piece by piece and repeat it.

5. Repeat step 4 with longer stretches.

6. Learners read along with the recording, keeping in step.

7. Learners read aloud the entire text by themselves with no audio support.

8. Discuss the text as a piece of discourse by asking key questions.

The following text illustrates the approach.

A guy walked into a bank in New York City // asking for a loan for $4,000 dollars. // "Well, // before we lend you the money // we are going to need some kind of security" // the bank teller said. // "No problem" // the man responded, // "Here are the keys to my car, // you'll see it, // it's a black Porsche parked in the back of the parking lot." // A few weeks later // the man returned // to pay off his loan. While he was paying it up, // along with the interest of $11 dollars, // the manager came over. // "Sir, // we are very happy to have your business, // but if you don't mind me asking, // after you left // we made some enquiries // and found out that you are a millionaire. // Why would you need to borrow $4,000 dollars?" // "Well, // the guy responded, // "it's quite simple, // where else can I park my car for three weeks in New York // for $11 dollars?"

Here are some examples of awareness-raising questions:

1. These two nouns both have participle clauses after them.

   New York City // asking for a loan for $4,000 dollars

   a _black Porsche_ parked in the back of the parking lot.

   Why is the first pronounced as two units and the second as one?

   (In the first, the –ing clause is an adverbial, it is about the man not the city, while in the second it modifies the noun.)

2. Why is only the first of the _to_ infinitive clauses a separate thought group?

   the man returned // to pay off his loan

   we are very happy to have your business

   (The _to_ infinitive clauses have different functions. The first is an adverbial, an infinitive of purpose, and the second complements the adjective.

Complements are always tighter in clause structure and tend not to have separate thought groups.)

Shadowing is a controlled activity, but it is much more than reading aloud. The iterative nature of the activity makes progress tangible and builds confidence. As a regular procedure, shadowing can make learners sensitive to grammatical structure and discourse-conditioned choices of grammar and phonology.

Complex Sentences and Tone

If grammar is concerned with the construction of sentences, discourse factors influence the selection of the components. There is always a choice for learners with advanced grammar. Contrast the two utterances below.

Sally got up. She went to the shop.

After Sally had got up, she went to the shop.

The second is complex because it features subordination as well as the past perfect. Both utterances mean exactly the same thing, but the second gives the impression of greater proficiency. The nature of complexity has been much debated (see Carter, 2007, in a special addition of *Applied Linguistics* devoted to complexity), but subordination is recognised as a key marker of it. Subordination allows clauses to be combined and stacked, often quite intricately. Phonologically, subordinate clauses tend to feature a rising tone, with the main clause having a falling tone. This is because the subordinate clause is typically background information, the given or obvious, setting the scene for the main message, the new or non-obvious. (For a fuller discussion of the given versus new distinction, see Levis, 2014; for more information on final intonation, see Chapters 3 and 5 in this volume.)

Very complex clauses with several layers of subordination are rare in speaking because the assembly task is so demanding in real-time communication. However, a combination of subordinate + main clause is common in many sentence types, a pedagogical favourite being the conditional, as noted earlier in the chapter. The following activity is a drill to practise the third conditional.

The third conditional has the form of an *if* clause, with the past perfect and a main clause with a past tense modal (*would, could*, etc.) + *have* + *–ed* form. The meaning is of a hypothetical past and a different result: *If I had studied harder at school* (rise), *I would have made college* (fall). The sheer length of the construction and the typical contractions of the auxiliaries make such sentences difficult to articulate. Advanced learners would be expected to deal with this and also incorporate a rise on the *if* clause.

Tell learners that you are going to feed them a story bit by bit. Emphasise that this story is finished and in the past. You will tell them part of the story and they must transform it into a third conditional sentence. Demonstrate with the beginning of the story.

John went to a disco. He met Susan.

    — *If John hadn't been to a disco* (rise), *he wouldn't have met Susan* (fall).

Nominate one student to transform your words. First make sure the grammar is right—this might take the student a couple of tries—and then get the student to repeat the well-formed sentence with the correct pitch changes. Next drill that sentence with the whole class. Go through the whole story, building up the suspense and stopping to get students to predict what will happen next.

John met Susan and they fell in love.

    — *If John hadn't met Susan* (rise), *they wouldn't have fallen in love* (fall).

They fell in love and they got married.

    — *If they hadn't fallen in love* (rise), *they wouldn't have got(ten) married* (fall).

They got married and went on honeymoon.

    — *If they hadn't got(ten) married* (rise), *they wouldn't have gone on honeymoon* (fall).

They went on honeymoon and visited Greece.

    — *If they hadn't gone on honeymoon* (rise), *they wouldn't have visited Greece* (fall).

They visited Greece and stayed on an island.

    — *If they hadn't visited Greece* (rise), *they wouldn't have stayed on an island* (fall).

They stayed on an island and hired a yacht.

    — *If they hadn't stayed on an island* (rise), *they wouldn't have hired a yacht* (fall).

They hired a yacht and sailed out to sea.

    — *If they hadn't hired a yacht* (rise), *they wouldn't have sailed out to sea* (fall).

They sailed out to sea and the yacht sank.

    — *If they hadn't sailed out to sea* (rise), *the yacht wouldn't have sunk* (fall).

The yacht sank and they both drowned.

    — *If the yacht hadn't sunk* (rise), *they wouldn't have both drowned* (fall).

(So they wouldn't have died if John hadn't gone to a disco!)

This is another controlled activity, and it shows that drills can be used at higher levels with complex language. It gives students the opportunity to use, and importantly say, language that might be a passive rather than active resource; that is, they have been exposed to it but never incorporate it into their speaking. Experience of complex language benefits grammar and pronunciation, the drilling procedure making a strong association between them. Indeed, a fluency component can be added if learners are asked to make their own chain stories from provocative sentence beginners such as *If I'd woken up with green hair this morning. . . .* This is a common textbook activity and can be slotted in neatly. At this stage learners should be prepared to handle both the grammar and pronunciation in an extended and personalised speaking opportunity, surely the perfect formula for an integrated lesson.

Exclamatives and Sentence Stress

Exclamatives are non-interrogative phrases or clauses headed by *what* or *how*, for example, *What a lovely day! What a strange guy he is! How careless of me! How much money they spent!* The exclamation mark signals their strong emotional overtones. Their grammar is deceptive, as the elements that follow *what/how* are syntactically constrained. For example, while *how* cannot modify a degree adverb like *very* or *really* in questions (e.g., *How very sensible is she?*), it can in an exclamative (e.g., *How very sensible she is!*) The pronunciation is marked to suit the involvement in three ways. First, the voice is pitched high on *what/how* in a high starting key. Second, *what* and *how* are stressed more strongly, like content words, than they typically would be in questions. Third, the impact word carries the main stress and carries a rise-fall tone.

> *What a **lovely** (rise-fall) day!*
>
> *What a **strange** (rise-fall) guy he is!*
>
> *How **careless** (rise-fall) of me!*
>
> *How much **money** (rise-fall) they spent!*

This combination of emotional force, non-canonical grammar, and strong stress and pitch movement makes exclamatives a prime area for advanced language work.

The approach taken here is storytelling, a technique that offers a rich context with a high affect factor. The teacher tells the following joke and asks learners to supply a punchline:

> Bill and Ted are driving through the countryside. They go in their speedy car through some fields full of sheep. Ted is driving and Bill is in the passenger seat. Ted looks out of the window and says, "What a lot of sheep there are in that field!" Bill glances out and replies, "Yes, there are 61 sheep there." Ted is amused by that

remark. He stops the car and counts the sheep. "1, 2, 3 . . . 61." 61 exactly! Wow! They get in the car and keep driving, a bit quicker now. They're zooming through the fields now. Ted looks out of the window again and says, "<u>How many sheep there are in that field!</u>" Bill turns his head to see the sheep go by and replies, "Yes, there are 73 sheep there." Ted is really surprised now. H stops the car and counts the sheep. "1, 2, 3 . . . 73." 73 exactly! Amazing! They get in the car and carry on, really motoring now. They're racing through the fields. Ted looks out of the window again and says, "<u>What a lot of sheep in that field!</u>" Bill eyes the sheep as they flash by and replies, "Yes, there are 105 sheep there." Ted is astounded now. He stops the car and counts the sheep. "1, 2, 3 . . . 105." 105 exactly! He says to Bill, "You're a genius! *How quickly you count!* How do you do it?" Bill replies, "It's easy. . . . I count the legs and divide by 4."

Then the teacher can exploit the language. First, the teacher should elicit the exclamative clauses, retelling the joke and pausing if necessary. The more students listen to the language, the better; the beauty of jokes is that they are highly repetitive and allow multiple exposures to the target language. The teacher could then write the language on the board and draw attention to the grammar and pronunciation before drilling it as isolated sentences. The challenge could be increased slightly by retelling the joke and pausing for students to supply the appropriate exclamative. The next step would be to practise the language and pronunciation in a controlled environment—here the textbook support is an ideal prop—before a free activity, as presented below.

Work in groups. Take turns reading out these scenarios. Respond with an exclamative for each.

Example

You have a thing about a girl at college and finally pluck up the courage to ask her for a date. You see her at the lunch break alone and get ready to approach her . . . when a handsome soccer player comes up, sits next to her, gives her a big kiss, and says, "I'm back, honey."

What bad luck that was!

How embarrassing that could have been!

What a let-down!

1. It's late at night and your car breaks down on a back road. You see a motel and walk there looking for help. The door is open, you walk in, and the door closes behind you immediately. The lights go off and you find you are locked in.

2. You move into a new apartment and keep having the same dream every night, about a box under the stairs. You decide to check this out, look under the stairs, and sure enough there is a box. You open it and find a manuscript written in a strange language.

The next step would be for students to choose one of the scenarios and take turns continuing and developing the story. When they finish their section, the others again have to respond with exclamatives. To illustrate with the original example:

You don't lose hope and decide to impress your true love. She is obviously a fan of soccer, so you take up soccer in a big way and train every day. You get your big break when the trainer tells you he wants to include you in the next big match— alongside that handsome rival.

How very lucky I am!

What an amazing game this is going to be!

How well everything is turning out!

The task cycle goes from introducing the language through a story, highlighting the grammar and pronunciation connection, practising the mechanics through your textbook, and then providing a fluency activity that gives learners a choice in response types while still encouraging the target language.

Conclusion

Three activities have been presented to demonstrate the key principle that, at an advanced level, discourse is the motivation for grammar and pronunciation, which are exploited as a system of choices to make utterances optimal. Teaching advanced learners thus goes way beyond making them able to communicate in the basic sense of being understood. Advanced grammar with the appropriate phonological contouring will raise learners' production to a point where higher level considerations such as style, humour, and creativity can be criterial. Grammar and pronunciation then definitely remain relevant in advanced instruction, and it is an integrated approach that is especially sensitive to the discourse factors that give them full expression.

Resources

Cruttenden, A. (2014). *Gimson's pronunciation of English* (8th ed.). Abingdon, England: Routledge.

> *This is not a book with teaching activities, but particularly in Chapter 11 on connected speech, there is insightful reference to the interplay between grammar, pronunciation, and discourse features.*

Gilbert, J. (2012). *Clear speech* (4th ed.). Cambridge, England: Cambridge University Press.

> *Chapter 15 on thought groups is especially germane to the discussion, with clear illustrations and lovely lesson ideas.*

Hewings, M. (2007). *English in pronunciation in use, advanced.* Cambridge, England: Cambridge University Press.

> *Many of the features in the second half of the book are discourse-based, including work on thought groups, and concepts are clearly explained with copious examples.*

Marks, J., & Bowen, T. (2012). *The pronunciation book.* Surrey, England: Delta.

> *This ingenious resource goes further than most in making the link between grammar and pronunciation; for example, it treats the word order of adverbials.*

Rimmer, W. (2007). Syntax and pronunciation. *Speak Out!, 37*, 5–7.

> *This is a discussion article that concentrates on suprasegmentals and higher level grammar.*

Swan, M. (2012). Grammar and pronunciation. *Speak Out!, 47*, 21–23.

> *An expert on pedagogical grammar, Swan stresses the connections between grammar and pronunciation (and listening) in this brief article.*

Swan, M., & Walter, C. (2011). Pronunciation for grammar [CD-ROM]. In *Oxford English grammar course.* Oxford, England: Oxford English Course.

> *An original idea to practise sounds and suprasegmental features alongside the three-level grammar course.*

References

Carter, R. (2007). Response to special issue of applied linguistics devoted to language creativity in everyday contexts. *Applied Linguistics, 28*, 597–608.

Cauldwell, R. (2013). *Phonology for listening.* Birmingham, England: Speech in Action.

Cruttenden, A. (2014). *Gimson's pronunciation of English* (8th ed.). Abingdon, England: Routledge.

Gilbert, J. (2014). Intonation is hard to teach. In L. Grant (Ed.), *Pronunciation myths* (pp. 107–136). Ann Arbor: University of Michigan Press.

Jenkins, J. (2000). *The phonology of English as an international language.* Oxford, England: Oxford University Press.

Larsen-Freeman, D. (2003). *Teaching language: From grammar to grammaring.* Boston, MA: Heinle.

Levis, J. (2005). Changing contexts and shifting paradigms in pronunciation teaching. *TESOL Quarterly, 39*, 369–377.

Levis, J. (2014). New and given information in English: Conflicting pedagogical models. *Speak Out!, 50*, 32–36.

Marks, J. (2014). Being trained and being prepared: Challenges for pronunciation teacher training. *Speak Out!, 50*, 59–62.

Marks, J., & Bowen, T. (2012). *The pronunciation book*. Surrey, England: Delta.

Rimmer, W. (2004). Grammar for advanced learners. *International House Journal, 17*, 15–16. Retrieved from http://ihjournal.com

Rimmer, W. (2013). Will we be using them in 60 years' time? The future as a matter of course books. *IH Journal, 34*. Retrieved from http://ihjournal.com

Rimmer, W. (2014, June). *Pronunciation: The one that got away*. Paper presented at the MATSDA conference, Liverpool, England.

Rimmer, W. (in press). Pronunciation worksheets. In *Cambridge English: Empower teachers' book*. Cambridge, England: Cambridge University Press.

Tilbury, A. (2008). Something on language awareness: Should teachers learn or acquire it? In A. Scott (Ed.), *Best practice in language teaching: An IH perspective* (pp. 78–86). London, England: International House World Organisation.

Tomlinson, B., & Masuhara, H. (2013). Survey review: Adult coursebooks. *ELT Journal, 67*, 233–249.

Walker, R. (2010). *Teaching the pronunciation of English as a lingua franca*. Oxford, England: Oxford University Press.

CHAPTER 10

The Pronunciation-Reading Connection

Minah Woo and Rebecca Price

For ESL students who have a very difficult time matching the sound inventory of their first languages (L1s) to English and then recognizing a totally new combination of sounds or different combinations of sounds, the process of identifying, sorting, and producing new sounds can be slow, arduous, and frustrating. Pronunciation training has always been recognized as a tool that seeks to improve the accuracy of the oral production while also fine-tuning listening skills. Because of extensive research in the way the language is learned, a new role for pronunciation training has emerged as a powerful tool to be used in the reading process; specifically, pronunciation training can facilitate the critical first step of phonemic awareness (recognizing and manipulating sounds) and phonics (assigning letters to those sounds). Recent research in the field of reading establishes a strong correlation between phonics instruction and successful reading. For ESL students, a necessary tool for learning phonemic awareness and phonics is pronunciation training, especially training focused on segmentals (vowels and consonants). However, pronunciation is usually not incorporated into an ESL reading curriculum.

Advances in technology are shedding new light onto how the brain reads, and based on these discoveries we can no longer ignore some of the components of reading instruction that were dismissed in the whole-language era. Baddeley's work on the working memory, specifically the phonological loop, gives insights into how languages are learned (Baddeley, Gathercole, & Papagno, 1998; Gathercole & Baddeley, 1990, 1993; Lecture, 2000). These studies show that the phonological loop plays a critical role as a language learning device for both first and second languages. The sounds enter the phonological loop, and through repeated experience of connecting specific sounds to meaning, this knowledge is transferred to the long-term memory, where it can be quickly and automatically accessed in the future. Researchers have found that the phonological loop plays an important role not only in spoken language, but also in reading (Castles & Coltheart, 2004; Perfetti & Bolger, 2004; Schild, Röder, & Friedrich, 2011). For reading comprehension to occur, all written materials must be converted into speech sounds in the phonological loop first. Even when we read silently, the brain is busy converting written print to sounds in the phonological loop in order to access the long-term memory where meaning can be extracted. Therefore, to comprehend what was just read, properly accessing the long-term memory through the phonological loop becomes an essential key in the reading process.

The reading process requires the mastery of two different operations: processing print and overall comprehension, deriving meaning from what was processed. Although the two processes must work in tandem, development of the skills does not occur simultaneously because they use two distinct processes. To process print, one uses bottom-up skills that focus on matching sounds with graphemes, and this is dependent on the ability to hear and discriminate the sounds, manipulate the sounds, match the sounds to the correct graphemes, and extract lexical information. For second language (L2) learners, these print-processing skills are intricately tied to pronunciation. In contrast, comprehension uses "general cognitive skills . . . building of a mental structure corresponding to a narrative or expository account [and] it involves the same cognitive mechanism and processes whether it is based on listening, reading, looking at picture stories, or watching silent films" (Walter, 2008, p. 455). In order to become a proficient reader, both operations must work seamlessly. Therefore, good reading instruction must pay attention to the skills that must be taught for the different operations. Birch and others discuss the historic focus on developing comprehension skills while ignoring the print processing skills to the detriment to L2 learners (Birch, 2007; Castles & Coltheart, 2004; Ehri, 2003; Herron, 2008; Koda, 2004; Walter, 2008). In this chapter, we focus on using pronunciation strategies to develop the bottom-up skills, which we divide into lower and mid-level processing skills.

Lower Level Reading Skills Development

The lower level reading skills include phonemic awareness and phonics. In the following sections, we define the two skills and suggest activities that can be incorporated in the classroom.

Phonemic Awareness

Phonemic awareness is the ability to recognize and manipulate sounds. This first step in language learning does not depend on written material. Phonemic awareness is singlehandedly the best indicator of future reading and academic success (Ehri, 2001;

Share, Jorm, Maclean, & Matthews, 1984; Turan & Gul, 2008). As children learn the sound systems of their first language, this process of filtering, sorting, and assigning proper language sounds occurs naturally. Young children learning a second language may have an easier time since the critical period for building sounds in their brains has not ended (Kuhl, 2010). However, as older children and adults try to learn a new language, the process of discriminating sounds becomes much more cumbersome, and phonics for nonnative speakers who do not have the English sound system stored is very difficult.

If languages are learned through the phonological loop, then hearing and saying the sounds correctly becomes the first and perhaps most critical step in learning a new language; thus, pronunciation becomes a critical component as students learn a new sound system. For example, many older learners cannot tell the difference between *hit* /hɪt/ and *heat* /hit/, either when they hear it or when they say it. Beginning to differentiate these minimal pairs and applying the correct sounds (or at least consistent sounds even though they aren't exact) are significant steps in the decoding/recoding process. Without pronunciation instruction, students may never hear the differences in these sounds or even hear that initial and final consonants are different in words like *toll* /toʊl/, *told* /toʊld/, and *toe* /toʊ/ or *thin* /θɪn/ and *tin* /tɪn/. Without the ability to differentiate these words, students will not have a place to store their learned vocabulary, if they can learn it at all.

Phonics

Phonics moves beyond the sounds of the language and involves matching phonemes to the corresponding letters, applying syllable-division rules, and identifying spelling patterns. However, phonics for nonnative English speakers who do not have the English sound system stored is very difficult; thus, pronunciation becomes a critical component in phonics as students learn a new sound system and the letters that are associated with those sounds. Unlike children, older L2 learners don't usually have years to develop phonemic awareness before learning to read. Therefore, in an L2 classroom, learners will be developing phonemic awareness and almost immediately start the phonics process by trying to attach these new sounds to letters through decoding or to attach letters to sounds through encoding. Both phonemic awareness and phonics deserve separate instructional attention and comprise various subskills; however, in reality, separating the two skills for purposes of instruction can be difficult as many L2 learners, especially those from alphabetic languages, use their L1 knowledge of alphabets and sounds to begin the process of establishing a code by matching the new sounds with letters.

It is important to keep in mind while developing phonics that L2 readers need a consistent phonological inventory, a complete set of allowed sounds of the language that distinguishes the phonemes of the new language. The phonological inventory for an L2 learner may never sound exactly the same as a native speaker's inventory, but the inventory should be recognizable to a native speaker and be self-consistent. Celce-Murcia, Brinton, and Goodwin (1996), in fact, advocate for learners to use a phonemic alphabet in order to catalog and separate the sounds of English. Pronunciation texts have long used the International Phonetic Alphabet (IPA) for this purpose. Having a "well-elaborated L2 phonological inventory in the long-term memory" (Walter, 2008, p. 456) is important because information in the phonological loop is subject to a rapid decay (1–2 seconds). If the phonemes of the text are not properly combined quickly enough, then the meaning of the words of just-read material cannot be extracted from the long-term memory accurately.

Almost inseparable at this point is for L2 learners to be "taught how an alphabetic orthography maps the phonemic structure of speech" (Ehri, 2001, p. 356); thus, they need to learn to match the new phonemic sounds to the English spelling system. For example, trial and error could eventually lead an L2 learner to conclude that the VCe* pattern in a word results in the vowel being pronounced as a long (tense) vowel as in *line* or *rope*; however, instruction in this rule will facilitate more efficient noticing and, therefore, correct and efficient decoding. Furthermore, studies show that teaching phonological awareness alone does not improve learning to read, and phonological awareness needs to be combined with instruction in spelling in order to improve success in reading (Bradley & Bryant, 1983, 1985).

Although many of the newer pronunciation books deemphasize segmentals and spelling, these skills should not be ignored. One author who has given us a clear example of learning the phonemes and tying them to spelling is Gilbert. These skills are presented in Gilbert's *Clear Speech From the Start* (2001) and *Clear Speech* (2005), in which students practice and develop pronunciation skills using simple content words that they may already use in oral speech. Of special note is Gilbert's systematic approach to introducing the vowel sounds. She begins with long vowel sounds and contrasts them with short and reduced vowel sounds along with the rules that govern these spelling patterns. Although almost all of the pronunciation books on the market include sections that highlight important and confusing vowel and consonant sounds, to achieve the goal of a precise and accurate phonological inventory, more attention needs to be devoted to the IPA, minimal pair contrasts, and overall spelling rules.

---

*VCe: Vowel-Consonant letter combination followed by the letter e, i.e., C a k e
    ↑↑↑
    VCe

Four Guiding Principles

Pronunciation skills for L2 readers are fundamental for the bottom or lower level skills that require development of a very basic lexicon and matching that lexicon to word-level tasks like hearing sounds and words; manipulating those sounds; matching graphemes to sounds; identifying and using spelling patterns; using probabilistic reasoning and rime/onset for identifying more common sounds, patterns, and spelling; and developing a supply of sight words that have been memorized. There are four principles teachers must keep in mind while working on developing bottom-level reading skills.

The first principle has to do with the *relationship between listening and speaking*. Listening must be practiced and developed for readers to successfully cultivate the discrimination skills that are needed for any phonological, morphological, or lexical development. There is reason to believe that listening skills can be enhanced when students begin to notice differences between sounds because of their articulatory attempts. In other words, students may not hear the final /s/ on the word *talks*, but with practice articulating this sound, students begin to be more attentive to the ending when listening and eventually can add that sound at the end of a word (see also Chapter 7). More difficult are vowels; however, practice articulating *cheap* /tʃip/ versus *chip* /tʃɪp/ raises awareness of the differences between these two vowel sounds and can increase receptive listening skills through productive practice. Hornberger (2003) further supports this by stating that comprehensible output is as important as comprehensible input in second language acquisition.

The second principle is *encoding*. Most phonics programs practice decoding, converting written print into sounds, before encoding, converting sounds into written letters. However, Herron (2008) develops an argument for starting with encoding. As with the listening/speaking debate, there is ample support that developing encoding skills will also help with the decoding process. She purports that "the process of learning to read should start with students constructing words—because this process requires them to pronounce words first" (p. 78).

The third principle at work is *recoding*. When a student reads and decodes, the symbols on the page are recoded into a phonemic form, whether out loud or silently. Using the correct phonemes requires that a connection has been made between the phonemes and graphemes of the target language. Pronunciation and spelling are at the heart of this process. An essential component of this principle that cannot be ignored is that of repetition. Repetition is a fundamental step for the connections made in the working memory to be transferred to the long-term memory. Based on neuroscientific and speech acquisition research, Kjellin (1999) advocates for the importance of repetition in language learning and recommends 50–100 repetitions to learn a new word. Another proponent of repetition, Nation (2001), asserts that a "spaced repetition results in more secure learning than masses repetition" (p. 79). A spaced repetition is repeating the material after some time has passed, with each repetition spaced further in time, versus a massed repetition, which is repeating the material over and over at the time it is introduced. Spaced repetition is a useful tool to ensure that the learned material is stored in the long-term memory. Examples of spaced repetition are activities such as delaying copying, read and look up, dicto-comp, and retelling stories (Nation, 2001).

Finally, at all times during L2 learning, *lexical development* is paramount. L2 learners do not always have a developed oral lexicon to access when decoding words. That is to say that students may successfully decode a word and never make a meaning connection because the students don't have the target word in their lexicon. Successful phonemic awareness and phonics instruction will allow learners to read by sounding out the text. L1 learners with rich oral vocabulary can at this time match the meaning to the text as long as they can properly sound out the text. However, L2 learners with far less learned vocabulary may still be at a loss for meaning even if they can sound out all the letters successfully. The necessity of constantly adding new vocabulary further complicates the reading process for L2 learners.

Students must develop automaticity with meaningful, useful vocabulary as they become more proficient decoders (see also Chapter 1). Considering the fact that by kindergarten native speakers develop an oral lexicon of 10,000 words, L2 learners are at a distinct disadvantage. Thus, lexical development must be included intentionally. This connection between vocabulary and phonics led Koda (2004) to conclude that vocabulary development and phonics training must occur simultaneously. Fundamental to this approach is that, yes, students will learn new vocabulary in class, but more than that, they will develop the bottom-up skills to begin learning new vocabulary on their own, a far more important skill, a process that is dependent on oral production and pronunciation.

Table 1 presents some activities for developing bottom-level reading skills. They are divided into phonemic and phonics/spelling practice. Keep in mind that the above principles underlie all these activities, and remember the critical role that pronunciation plays for L2 learners. They must be able to hear the sounds and pronounce the sounds properly in order for these activities to be meaningful. These are just a few ideas to get you started!

Table 1 Activities for Bottom-Level Skills Development

ACTIVITY IDEAS	EXAMPLE ACTIVITIES
Phonemic practice	
• Use listening practice to differentiate specific phonemes, words containing the taught phonemes, spelling patterns, and sight words.	• Use manipulatives such as letters on index cards, refrigerator magnet letters, or toy block letters and have students make letters or words they hear. You can also create a fun manipulative using Legos. Write letters on the sides of the Legos and have students form words by putting Lego pieces together (see http://thisreadingmama.com/spelling-with-lego-letters). See Chapter 11 for more activities.
• Give frequent dictation practice involving specific phonemes, words containing the taught phonemes, spelling patterns, and sight words.	• Give each student a white board for dictation practice, and have them write what they hear. You can dictate words or sentences. Make sure you don't over-accentuate or say the sentence too slowly. If working on one word, you can also practice phonemic addition, deletion, and substitution (e.g., write *top*, then write *stop*, then write *step*).
• Practice recognizing and producing minimal pairs, orally and aurally.	• Print out minimal pair words and have students hold up the one they hear. Have students take turns saying one while other students vote on what they have heard. This works on both oral and aural acquisition of the sound.
• Practice recognizing and producing rime/onset patterns and rhymes.	• Create a word family wall (e.g., list of words that begin with *st–*, list of words that end in *–at*; for more activities, see Chapter 1).
Phonics/spelling practice	
• Develop grapheme knowledge of all of the phonemes taught—decode and encode. • Practice decoding and encoding words that are consistent with phonics rules.	• Play a fly swatter game with all the letters of the alphabet on the board haphazardly arranged. Say a sound and have students swat the corresponding letter. First one to swat the letter wins. (grapheme knowledge) • Have all students come up to the board (each given a little space and something to write with). Dictate words and have students write them down. At the count of three, everyone turns around and compares the answers. If you don't have enough board space, it can also be done with individual white boards and students sitting in a circle. (encoding) • Have different words printed on paper and taped around the room. Say the words and have students run to the right word. If you have a lot of students and have room in the classroom, you can have multiple words at different locations to avoid overcrowding. (decoding)

continued

• Develop spelling rules starting with basic consonants, vowels, and syllables. • Introduce word stress rules, and practice hearing and applying them to all new words. • Introduce simple morphemes (e.g., *s, ing, ly, un*), and practice attaching them to words that have been learned with special attention to word stress.	• Teach syllable stress and the syllable division every time a new word is learned. Note syllable divisions and stresses to all words in the dictionary (for more activities, see Chapter 12).
• Practice blending CC (consonant consonant) and CCC (consonant consonant consonant)words (see Chapters 1 and 7 for more information on consonant clusters).	• Chant and add additional letters to consonant blends (e.g., *ing, ring, pring, spring*) while keeping to a beat. It's okay to practice with nonsense words because the key is pronouncing them correctly while keeping to the beat.
• Develop a list of sight words that are necessary but for which the phonics rules to not apply.	• Create a word wall. A fun idea is to do this with a most frequently used word list (e.g., General Service List, Dolch Words, Fry's List) and rank them (section for 1–500 commonly used words, 501–1000 commonly used words, etc.) • For words that are harder to memorize, students can draw pictures to depict the words and create a word art wall. This works especially well for visual learners.  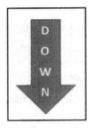

Mid-Level Reading Skills Development

While lower level skill development focuses more on word recognition skills, mid-level skill development involves practice with multisyllabic words, phrases, and sentences. Table 2 presents some activities for developing mid-level reading skills. Keeping in mind that lower level skills are a necessary prerequisite, instructors can help L2 readers tackle longer language units and move closer to the automatic processing required for comprehension of larger, more complex units of language. At this phase, readers become more attentive to longer words, phrases, and sentence-level language and the use of function words, collocations, phrasing, punctuation, intonation, and grammar. The working memory is limited in capacity, and properly processing the written text into chunks frees up more cognitive resources to devote to comprehension.

Pronunciation activities associated with suprasegmentals focus on thought groups, pauses, word stress in multisyllabic words, word stress related to more complicated morphological structures, sentence stress and de-stress (content and function words together), and pragmatics. These pronunciation activities, which are thoroughly covered in almost all of the pronunciation textbooks of the last 10 years, align closely with the mid-level reading skills that students need.

Table 2   Activities for Mid-Level Skills Development

ACTIVITY IDEAS	EXAMPLE ACTIVITIES
• Develop awareness of thought groups and collocations through listening, reading, and pronunciation activities. • Teach syllable division rules, and apply stress rules and vowel lengthening and reduction rules to multisyllabic words (see Chapter 2 for more ideas). • Practice morphemic additions to words, and apply stress rules and vowel lengthening and reduction rules to multisyllabic words.	• Use resources such as jazz chants, poetry, nursery rhymes, and simple dialogues to practice combining and connecting longer pieces of speech. While listening to the teacher recite the passage, students can mark their copy with the appropriate thought groups and collocations. Students practice by doing choral (whole class reading together) and shadow readings (reading in a quiet voice immediately following the teacher). • Students must first be able to hear the syllable beats that occur in words. Say a word and have students vote with their fingers the number of syllables they hear. Teach students the rules using a spelling book as a resource. • Group new words on a chart by the number of syllables and the syllable stress patterns. (e.g., three syllables with the middle stress syllable: O—O, three syllables with the initial stress syllable: —OO; for more activity suggestions, see Chapters 1 and 2).

Higher Level Reading Skills Development

Higher-level reading skills, also called top-down skills, apply cognitive faculties developed through life and educational experiences. Top-down skills incorporate background knowledge, inferencing, predicting, categorizing, and critical thinking to analyze the text. In order to perform these higher order thinking skills, cognitive resources must be freed up. Students with well-developed bottom-up skills can "activate [the] pronunciation and meaning immediately in memory [which allows them] . . . to focus their attention on comprehension rather than word recognition" (Ehri, 2014, p. 5). To reiterate, the critical point to make in this chapter is that automaticity of the lower and mid-level skills allow the brain to devote more cognitive resources to these higher order thinking skills that are critical if a learner is to move beyond basic word interpretation reading. An emphasis on these upper level skills without developing the lower and mid-level skills can lead to frustration and discouragement with the reading process. Often, the lower and mid-level skills are dismissed as beginner skills and are not addressed in intermediate and advanced classes. The bottom-up reading strategies are no longer limited to the early stages of reading, but should be a crucial component of good reading instruction at all levels (Nassaji, 2003; Walter, 2008). If an advanced L2 learner is struggling with reading comprehension, it is most likely the breakdown or gaps in the lower and mid-level skills that hinder phonological processing required to access the long-term memory.

Conclusion

While the L1 oral language is acquired naturally, reading is a human-made invention (Wolf, 2007) and has to be learned for both L1 and L2 readers. The process of becoming a successful reader is difficult because of the two processes that must be learned separately and then be applied simultaneously. A successful reader can use bottom-up and mid-level reading skills to process print with automaticity and also use top-down skills such as skimming, scanning, and summarizing to process the meaning of the text. These two processes must work seamlessly and simultaneously to reach the goal of reading comprehension. However, for L2 learners, there is an added layer of difficulty that makes the already arduous task of learning to read even more complex. While L1 learners' oral language is developed naturally, L2 learners must develop this at the same time they are developing their reading skills. Also, L2 learners may already have top-down skills that are cognitive skills, not literacy skills, developed from their prior educational experience (Carrell, 1991; Cheung, 2007; Walter, 2008).

Alderson (1984) asked, "Is second language reading a language problem or a reading problem?" (p. 1). When teaching reading to L2 learners, teachers must first consider the student's L1 reading ability and L2 language proficiency. The answers to Alderson's question will guide teachers in choosing the proper methodology in teaching L2 reading. For example, young students with no L1 reading background and no L2 English oral proficiency will need to develop oral language and decoding skills first and build in reading comprehension skills. Adult learners who are well educated in their L1 will already have a well-developed comprehension system and many years of practicing these upper level skills in their L1. They do not need activities to learn this cognitive process that is already in place, and targeted instruction on lower and mid-level skills will fill in the gap in order for the comprehension process in the L2 to be efficient. While not ignoring the importance of the top-down skills, this chapter has discussed why building lower and mid-level skills is important for L2 learners. Underlying all of these principles is the important role that pronunciation plays in L2 reading acquisition. "All in all, it seems reasonable to conclude that phonological decoding is perhaps the most indispensable competence for reading acquisition in all languages" (Koda, 2004, p. 34). Direct pronunciation instruction that will enable the proper phonological decoding to take place will increase L2 readers' processing efficiency and fluency.

Resources

Baddeley, A., Gathercole, S., & Papagno, C. (1998). The phonological loop as a language learning device. *Psychological Review, 105*(1), 158–173.

Birch, B. M. (2007). *English L2 reading: Getting to the bottom.* Mahwah NJ: Routledge.

Celce-Murcia, M., Brinton, D. M., & Goodwin, J. M. (1996). *Teaching pronunciation: A reference for teachers of English to speakers of other languages.* New York, NY: Cambridge University Press.

Gilbert, J. B. (2005). *Clear speech.* New York, NY: Cambridge University Press.

Koda, K. (2004). *Insights into second language reading: A cross-linguistic approach.* New York, NY: Cambridge University Press.

Wolf, M. (2007). *Proust and the squid: The story and science of the reading brain.* New York, NY: HarperCollins.

References

Alderson, C. J. (1984). Reading in a foreign language: A reading problem or a language problem? In C. J. Alderson & A. H. Urguhart (Eds.), *Reading in a foreign language* (pp. 1–27). London, England: Longman.

Baddeley, A., Gathercole, S., & Papagno, C. (1998). The phonological loop as a language learning device. *Psychological Review, 105*(1), 158–173.

Birch, B. M. (2007). *English L2 reading: Getting to the bottom.* Mahwah, NJ: Routledge.

Bradley, L., & Bryant, P. (1983). Categorizing sounds and learning to read: A causal connection. *Nature, 301*, 419–421.

Bradley, L., & Bryant, P. (1985). *Rhyme and reason in reading and spelling.* Ann Arbor: University of Michigan Press.

Carrell, P. L. (1991). Second language reading: Reading ability or language proficiency? *Applied Linguistics, 12*(2), 159–179.

Castles, A., & Coltheart, M. (2004). Is there a causal link from phonological awareness to success in learning to read? *Cognition, 18,* 77–111.

Celce-Murcia, M., Brinton, D. M., & Goodwin, J. M. (1996). *Teaching pronunciation: A reference for teachers of English to speakers of other languages.* New York, NY: Cambridge University Press.

Cheung, H. (2007). The role of phonological awareness in mediating between reading and listening to speech. *Language and Cognitive Processes, 22,* 130–154.

Ehri, L. C. (2001). The development of spelling knowledge and its role in reading acquisition and reading disability. *Journal of Learning Disabilities, 22,* 356–365.

Ehri, L. C. (2003). *Systematic phonics instruction: Findings of the National Reading Panel.* Paper presented at the invitational seminar organized by the Standards and Effectiveness Unit, Department for Education and Skills, British Government. (ERIC Document Reproduction Service No. ED479646)

Ehri, L. C. (2014). Orthographic mapping in the acquisition of sight word reading, spelling memory, and vocabulary learning. *Scientific Studies of Reading, 18,* 5–21.

Gathercole, S. E., & Baddeley, A. D. (1990). Phonological memory deficits in language disordered children: Is there a causal connection? *Journal of Memory & Language, 29,* 336–360.

Gathercole, S. E., & Baddeley, A. D. (1993). Phonological working memory: A critical building block for reading development and vocabulary acquisition? *European Journal of the Psychology of Education, 8,* 259–272.

Gilbert, J. B. (2001). *Clear speech from the start.* New York, NY: Cambridge University Press.

Gilbert, J. B. (2005). *Clear speech.* New York, NY: Cambridge University Press.

Herron, J. (2008, September). Why phonics teaching must change. *Educational Leadership,* pp. 77–81.

Hornberger, N. H. (2003). Continua of biliteracy. In N. H. Hornberger (Ed), *Continua of biliteracy: An ecological framework for educational policy, research, and practice in multilingual settings* (pp. 3–34). Tonawanda, NY: Multilingual Matters.

Kjellin, O. (1999). Accent addition: Prosody and perception facilitates second language learning. In O. Fujimura, B. D. Joseph, & B. Palek (Eds.), *Proceedings of LP'98 Linguistics and Phonetics Conference: Vol. 2* (pp. 373–398). Columbus, OH: Karolinum Press.

Koda, K. (2004). *Insights into second language reading: A cross-linguistic approach.* New York, NY: Cambridge University Press.

Kuhl, P. K. (2010). Brain mechanisms in early language acquisition. *Neuron, 67,* 713–727.

Lecture, M. K. (2000). How does the brain learn language? Insight from the study of children with and without language impairment. *Developmental Medicine & Child Neurology, 42,* 133–142.

Nassaji, H. (2003). Higher-level and lower-level text processing skills in advanced ESL reading comprehension. *Modern Language Journal, 87,* 261–276.

Nation, I. S. P. (2001). *Learning vocabulary in another language.* New York, NY: Cambridge University Press.

Perfetti, C. A., & Bolger, D. A. (2004). The brain might read that way. *Scientific Studies of Reading, 8,* 293–304.

Schild, U., Röder, B., & Friedrich, C. K. (2011). Learning to read shapes the activation of neural lexical representations in the speech recognition pathway. *Developmental Cognitive Neuroscience, 1,* 163–174.

Share, D. L., Jorm, A. F., Maclean, R., & Matthews, R. (1984). Sources of individual differences in reading acquisition. *Journal of Educational Psychology, 76,* 1309–1324.

Turan, F., & Gul, G. (2008). Early precursor of reading: Acquisition of phonological awareness skills. *Educational Sciences: Theory & Practice, 8,* 279–284.

Walter, C. (2008). Phonology in second language reading: not an optional extra. *TESOL Quarterly, 42,* 455–474.

Wolf, M. (2007). *Proust and the squid: The story and science of the reading brain.* New York, NY: HarperCollins.

CHAPTER 11

Integrating Pronunciation Instruction With Passage-Level Reading Instruction

Feifei Han

The sound system of English lays the basis for a successful mastery of other skills, namely listening, speaking, reading, and writing (Celce-Murcia, Brinton, & Goodwin, 2010). Among the four skills, listening and speaking abilities depend heavily on abilities of perceiving and producing correct sound systems. Even for the reading and writing abilities, which may initially seem to have a limited relationship with pronunciation, to master the two skills requires in-depth understanding of the English writing system, which maps speech sound (the phonological system) onto basic linguistic units (the orthographical system; Yamashita, 2013). One of the apparent advantages of integrating teaching pronunciation with the four skills lies in the fact that the sound system is closely associated with the every aspect of the four skills and pronunciation itself is a rich resource "for creating meaning and for expressing a variety of functions" (Celce-Murcia et al., 2010, p. 365). Hence, a properly designed integrative pronunciation curriculum will not only solve the problems associated with limited time allocated to teaching pronunciation, it may also enhance pronunciation and the four skills simultaneously. As a result of this dual enhancement of pronunciation and the other four skills, learners will find themselves functioning more flexibly in real communicative scenarios. The focus of this chapter is on how to integrate pronunciation instruction with passage-level reading instruction.

Reading instruction has always been given more attention than other skills because reading functions not only a skill, but also as the most important source of language input for English language learners (Dubin & Bycina, 1991). Therefore, integrating pronunciation and reading instruction is a promising solution to the problem of the lack of time experienced by teachers who do not have a separate session to devote to pronunciation but whose students need help with pronunciation. The reason for combining reading and pronunciation, however, is not as straightforward as the reason for integrating pronunciation with other skills. Nonetheless, according to Birch (2014) and Pressley and Allington (2014), bringing pronunciation into the reading curriculum can have beneficial results.

Reading is a very complex cognitive activity (Shiotsu, 2009), especially reading in a foreign language. In order for English language learners to achieve a good grasp of English reading skills, they need to understand the correspondence between English phonology and English orthography. Having a certain level of understanding of how speech sound maps to the spelling of a word enables learners to identify a word (known as word recognition) when they read (Shiotsu, 2009). Word recognition is the most frequently "recurring cognitive activity" in reading (Perfetti, 2007, p. 357). There is general agreement among researchers that it is impossible for fluent reading to take place without accurate and fast word recognition (Koda, 2005). From this perspective, activities that target the articulation of single letters, letter combinations, real words, and pseudo-words may also increase the speed of English word identification. For teachers who are interested in combining pronunciation instruction with word-level reading, please see Chapter 10 in this volume.

However, past research has consistently reported that training of word identification skills at word level often fails to contribute to improved comprehension (National Reading Panel, 2000), even though such training enhances word recognition speed and accuracy (e.g., Akamatsu, 2008). In contrast, training methods that are directed toward reading connected texts often leads to an increased level of comprehension of the training materials, and after the training, readers are also able to transfer the increased comprehension ability to reading novel texts (e.g., Martin-Chang & Levy, 2005). There are three major types of passage-level reading training methods: extensive, speed, and repeated (Macalister, 2010). Each of the methods can potentially be integrated with pronunciation instruction. The following section discusses some activities that combine teaching pronunciation and passage-level reading.

Extensive Reading and Pronunciation Instruction

Extensive reading is a pedagogy that encourages learners to read a large amount of materials (Yamashita, 2013). Extensive reading "means reading in quantity and in order to gain a general understanding of what is read. It is intended to develop good reading habits, to build up knowledge of vocabulary and structure, and to encourage a liking for reading" (Richards & Schmidt, 2002, pp. 193–194). In a typical extensive reading class, students are able to choose what they want to read from a vast amount of reading materials on a wide range of topics at different levels of difficulty without teachers' explicit instruction (Day & Bamford, 2002). The following activities, *Read Aloud and Identify* and *Sort Out and Categorize*, can be used for combining extensive reading and pronunciation instruction.

Read Aloud and Identify

This is an activity in which one student reads aloud at a time, and the rest of the students listen and identify pronunciation problems. In an extensive reading class, the teacher can ask learners to spend the majority of the time reading on their own. At the end of the lesson, the teacher can ask each student to read one page or one paragraph of what they have been reading aloud in front of the class while focusing on one aspect of pronunciation that was pretaught. For instance, teachers may want to encourage students to break the passage into appropriate thought groups or to focus on applying the correct word stress to all of the multisyllabic words in the passage. Before students read, they should be given time to mark a copy of their passage to make reading aloud easier, and they should practice quietly to themselves. This step may also be assigned for homework to ensure all students have ample time to correctly mark the passage and for practice. While a student is reading, the rest of the class need to pay close attention to his/her pronunciation and note down any inaccurate pronunciation on a copy of the text. For instance, if the focus is on using appropriate thought groups, the listeners could mark the thought groups they hear. After the reading, the pausing choices of the speaker could be discussed and alternatives suggested. Similarly, if the focus is on word stress, listeners could write down or highlight words they think are stressed incorrectly. After each discussion, teachers can summarize any pronunciation inconsistencies on the board and then model the phrase accurately and ask students to read, imitate, and correct their own.

Sort Out and Categorize

This is an activity that requires learners to find examples of words containing the same pronunciation of different vowels. Although this can be done as a word-level reading activity, it is easily adapted as a supplement reading activity by putting it in an extensive reading class. In an extensive reading class, teachers can allocate a certain amount of time for learners to find examples of a vowel sound in the text they have read in the class and to sort out how many different spellings they may have for the same sound. For instance, for /i/, the letter combinations of *ea* (*meat*) and *ee* (*teeth*) are pronounced as /i/. Teachers may also put students into groups and give each group a particular vowel or diphthong. Learners provide as many examples as possible from the texts they have read and write them down. In the end, each group can show the whole class what words have appeared in their reading texts. Students may also benefit from the summaries done by the other groups. Moreover, doing this activity may raise learners' awareness that there is no one-to-one correspondence between a sound and a letter. This awareness is important in increasing students' word decoding efficiency, which itself lays a foundation to fluent reading of passages that are formed by individual words. With enhanced word decoding efficiency, students' limited working memory capacity that is predominantly occupied by slow word decoding can now be used largely to construct a coherent interpretation of the text; hence, passage-level comprehension will be boosted. To learn more about possibilities of combining pronunciation instruction with word-level reading, please see Chapter 10.

Speed Reading and Pronunciation Instruction

According to Macalister (2010), a speed reading course normally consists of "a set number of texts of a fixed length, written within a restricted lexicon, followed by several multi-choice questions" (p. 105). The reason for using restricted vocabulary in the reading texts is because the majority of words are expected to be known by readers. Therefore, readers tend to perform the reading tasks at a faster pace than their normal speed, while at the same time focusing on comprehension. Through reading a large number of texts with restricted vocabulary and grammatical structures that students are familiar with, students' focus can be shifted from worrying about new words and novel grammatical features to reading speed. Hence, their reading speed is more likely to be increased. In addition, Tran and Nation (2014) found that an increase in a learner's rate of reading correlates with an increase in language memory span. Speed reading activities can also incorporate pronunciation instruction. The following activities are sample activities to illustrate the possibility of such integration.

Read as Quickly as You Can

This is an activity for practicing pronunciation, which can also form part of a speed reading course. At the beginning of class, the teacher can ask students to read one or two selected texts and to write down how much time they have spent on reading the texts. Then students are asked to read the text again in their preferred way (either silent reading or reading aloud) in order to answer comprehension questions created by the teacher. After students finish a comprehension reading task, the teacher can ask each student to read the same preselected paragraph aloud several times, and each time the student or teacher should keep a record of the time spent on reading the paragraph. Students need to read as accurately as possible while also increasing their reading speed. The teacher should remind them to pay close attention to several aspects of prosody: clearly and correctly articulating the peak vowel of stressed content words, linking and blending between words, and breaking speech down into thought groups with appropriate final intonation. Interestingly, as students become more proficient at de-stressing the function words in the text and linking and blending when possible, the rate of reading actually increases because they are not clearly reading each word and they have reduced the pausing time between words. However, by applying thought group patterns appropriately, they are still comprehensible. In the end, the top three students with the fastest reading times could be rewarded by the teacher.

This exercise aims to enhance learners' reading fluency, which refers to comprehending a text at an appropriate rate (Hudson, Pullen, Lane, & Torgesen, 2009). Adopting a componential perspective to understanding reading fluency, researchers maintain that the most important components involved in fluent reading are decoding accuracy, word recognition automaticity, and appropriate prosody (Kuhn & Stahl, 2003). As successfully using proper prosodic features when reading aloud has been shown as a critical indicator of fluency reading (Kuhn, Schwanenflugel, & Meisinger, 2010), the current activity is a good combination of exercising suprasegmental features of pronunciation and practicing reading fluency at the passage level. Instead of asking students to read individual words, this activity requires that they read a connected text aloud, which not only creates opportunities for learners to use proper prosody, an important feature for reading fluency, but also gives teachers chances to address the inappropriate prosodic features. Through reading aloud as quickly as possible, both reading fluency and pronunciation skills are exercised in a single drill.

Repeated Reading and Pronunciation Instruction

Repeated reading, as suggested by its name, refers to reading a text more than once. It is one of the most frequently used training methods in enhancing reading fluency in first language reading (Samuels, 1979). Repeated reading may take a variety of forms, including unassisted repeated reading, which involves reading the same text a number of times without using a model text (e.g., Samuels, 1979); assisted repeated reading, which involves using prepared audio materials as a model for learners (e.g., Chomsky, 1976); paired reading, whereby a pair of students takes turns repeating the same text (e.g., Topping, 1987); and echo reading, in which the teacher reads the text aloud first and then asks learners to imitate or to echo (e.g., Mathes, Torgesen, & Allor, 2001). These methods have some features in common. First, they require learners to read aloud rather than to read silently. Second, the passages for practice are normally short, which encourages repetition over an extended period. Third, an essential component of these methods is feedback on students' performance, either from teachers or from peers (Jeon, 2009). Research has consistently reported that repeated reading has dual effects on oral reading fluency development and reading comprehension (National Reading Panel, 2000; Stahl & Heubach, 2005). The positive effect of improved reading ability gained in repeatedly reading the same materials can be transferable to reading new passages (Therrien, Wickstrom, & Jones, 2006). This means that repeated reading instruction can be altered in some way to incorporate pronunciation instruction in English language teaching. Below are a couple of exercises for teachers to adapt for use in an English class where reading instruction plays a central role and pronunciation serves as a complementary focus.

Who Is the Best Follower?

This activity (also known as a mirroring activity) is suitable for an assisted repeated reading class, a special form of repeated reading that requires some model texts to be used as assistance for students. This activity requires teachers to prepare texts that are suitable for learners to carry out repeated readings. This means that the grammatical features and the level of vocabulary should not pose a challenge to learners. Teachers need to prepare a good-quality model audio recording, in which a proficient English speaker reads the text aloud with clear pronunciation, including the correct stress, intonation, and pauses. When the repeated reading session begins, the teacher plays the model text, sentence by sentence, and asks students to read after the model. Learners should be instructed to try their best to imitate the pronunciation in the audio recording. The teacher can play the recording a few times, which gives students ample opportunities to repeatedly read the same text aloud. In the end, the teacher asks every student to stand up to read the same part of the text. Then the teacher and students together can offer feedback about a pretaught target aspect of the speaker's pronunciation in terms of how similar it is to the pronunciation in the audio file. If more than one aspect is to be focused on, listeners can divide the pronunciation targets so that each student is listening for one target, such as word stress, prominence, or linking. In this way, the feedback is more targeted and listeners are not overwhelmed by trying to listen for too many things. Alternatively, this activity can be used as homework. Students can take the recording home and imitate the pronunciation and prosodic features of the audio file. After practice, they can have their own read-aloud recorded and sent to the teacher for evaluation. The teacher will then discover with "the best follower," who shows the best imitation of the pronunciation on the recording. See Chapter 9 for more shadowing activities.

Echo Me, Please

This activity offers the possibility of combining echo reading and pronunciation practice. It is different from *Who Is the Best Follower?*, in which students play a peripheral role when following the audio recording. In *Echo Me, Please*, every student is able to play a leading role. This activity can be undertaken as pair work. Students are paired by the teacher, and the teacher assigns each student in the pair a different text. Students are first given the opportunity to repeatedly read their own material quietly to themselves in order to become familiar with it. During this preparation time, they can mark up their text with stress, linking, and intonation symbols so as to help them read more fluently and to highlight the target pronunciation structure. Then within each pair, students take turns reading aloud while the other student echoes. Students should repeat this echoing process until both of them think their partner has a good mastery of reading the text. In the echoing process, the teacher needs to remind students to focus their attention on correctly pronouncing a single target feature, such as a particular troublesome consonant or vowel sound or an aspect of prosody. In the case of any discrepancies, students can raise their hand to ask the teacher to resolve the issue. In this way, students can improve their pronunciation in terms of both segmental and suprasegmental features through scaffolding and help from the teacher. As was mentioned previously, while good mastery of the segmental aspect of pronunciation is essential in mapping phonological codes onto linguistic units, which necessitates accurate and fast word identification skills, using appropriate suprasegmental elements in reading is a key indicator of fluent reading. This activity therefore is able to increase students' reading fluency from the two aspects.

Conclusion

The above activities are only a few examples of integrating pronunciation and reading instruction. It is hoped that these sample activities will open a door for English language teachers, curricula designers, and materials writers to generate more thoughtful and interesting activities that help learners practice pronunciation at the same time as enhancing their reading skills. Below are some suggestions for further readings, which may contribute to an in-depth understanding of how to implement teaching pronunciation in an English teaching classroom and may encourage insightful and creative ideas for how to strategically combine pronunciation instruction in time-constrained English classes.

Resources

Celce-Murcia, M., Brinton, D., & Goodwin, J. (2010). *Teaching pronunciation: A course book and reference guide.* New York, NY: Cambridge University Press.

Grice, M., & Stefan, B. (2007). An introduction to intonation: Functions and models. In J. Trouvain & U. Gut (Eds.), *Non-native prosody: Phonetic description and teaching practice* (pp. 25–51). Berlin, Germany: Walter De Gruyter.

Gut, U., Trouvain, J., & Barry, W. (2007). Bridging research on phonetic descriptions with knowledge from teaching practice the case of prosody in non-native speech. In J. Trouvain & U. Gut (Eds.), *Non-native prosody: Phonetic description and teaching practice* (pp. 3–21). Berlin, Germany: Walter De Gruyter.

References

Akamatsu, N. (2008). The effects of training on automatization of word recognition in English as a foreign language. *Applied Psycholinguistics, 29,* 175–193.

Birch, B. M. (2014). *English L2 reading: Getting to the bottom* (2nd ed.). Mahwah, NJ: Lawrence Erlbaum.

Celce-Murcia, M., Brinton, D., & Goodwin, J. (2010). *Teaching pronunciation: A course book and reference guide.* New York, NY: Cambridge University Press.

Chomsky, C. (1976). After decoding: What. *Language Arts, 53,* 288–296.

Day, R., & Bamford, J. (2002). Top ten principles for teaching extensive reading. *Reading in a Foreign Language, 14,* 136–141. Retrieved from http://nflrc.hawaii.edu/rfl

Dubin, F., & Bycina, D. (1991). Academic reading and the ESL/EFL teachers. In M. Celce-Murcia (Ed.), *Teaching English as a second or foreign language* (pp. 195–215). Rowley, MA: Newbury House.

Hudson, R. F., Pullen, P. C., Lane, H. B., & Torgesen, J. K. (2009). The complex nature of reading fluency: A multidimensional view. *Reading and Writing Quarterly, 25,* 4–32.

Jeon, E. H. (2009). Oral reading fluency in second language reading. *Reading in a Foreign Language, 24,* 186–208.

Koda, K. (2005). *Insights into second language reading: A cross-linguistic approach.* New York, NY: Cambridge University Press.

Kuhn, M. R., Schwanenflugel, P. J., & Meisinger, E. B. (2010). Aligning theory and assessment of reading fluency: Automaticity, prosody, and definitions of fluency. *Reading Research Quarterly, 45,* 230–251.

Kuhn, M. R., & Stahl, S. A. (2003). Fluency: A review of developmental and remedial practices. *Journal of Educational Psychology, 95,* 3–21.

Macalister, J. (2010). Speed reading courses and their effect on reading authentic texts: A preliminary investigation. *Reading in a Foreign Language, 22,* 104–116.

Martin-Chang, S., & Levy, B. (2005). Fluency transfer: Differential gains in reading speed and accuracy following isolated word and context training. *Reading and Writing, 18,* 343–376.

Mathes, P. G., Torgesen, J. K., & Allor, J. H. (2001). The effects of peer assisted learning strategies for first grader readers with and without computer assisted instruction in phonological awareness. *American Educational Research Journal, 38,* 371–410.

National Reading Panel. (2000). *Reports of the subgroups.* Washington, DC: National Institute of Child Health and Development.

Perfetti, C. A. (2007). Reading ability: Lexical quality to comprehension. *Scientific Studies of Reading, 11,* 357–383.

Pressley, M., & Allington, R. (2014). *Reading instruction that works: The case for balanced teaching* (4th ed.). New York, NY: Guilford Press.

Richards, J. C., & Schmidt, R. (2002). *Longman dictionary of language teaching and applied linguistics* (3rd ed.). London, England: Pearson Education.

Samuels, S. J. (1979). The method of repeated readings. *The Reading Teacher, 32,* 403–408.

Shiotsu, T. (2009). Reading ability and components of word recognition speed: The case of L1-Japanese EFL learners. In Z. Han & N. Anderson (Eds.), *Second language reading research and instruction* (pp. 15–37). Ann Arbor: University of Michigan Press.

Stahl, S. A., & Heubach, K. (2005). Fluency-oriented reading instruction. *Journal of Literacy Research, 37,* 25–60.

Therrien, W., Wickstrom, K., & Jones, K. (2006). Effect of a combined repeated reading and question generation intervention on reading achievement. *Learning Disabilities Research and Practice, 21,* 89–97.

Topping, K. (1987). Paired reading: A powerful technique for parent use. *The Reading Teacher, 40,* 608–614.

Tran, T. N. Y, & Nation, P. (2014). Reading speed improvement in a speed reading course and its effect on language memory span. *Electronic Journal of Foreign Language Teaching, 11,* 5–20.

Yamashita, J. (2013). Word recognition subcomponents and passage level reading in a foreign language. *Reading in a Foreign Language, 25,* 52–71.

CHAPTER 12

Integrating Pronunciation With Spelling and Punctuation

Adam Brown

The Alphabetic Principle

Linguists categorise spelling systems into three types. In logographic systems, such as the one used for Chinese, symbols (characters) in the writing represent whole linguistic units (words) and often constituent parts of words (morphemes). In syllabaries, such as the Japanese *kana* system, symbols in the spelling represent whole syllables. In an alphabetic system, letters in the spelling represent individual vowel or consonant sounds (phonemes). This is the most common type of spelling system, although the alphabet that is used may vary. English and many other languages use the Roman alphabet, sometimes with slight variations, but other alphabets exist, such as Cyrillic (for Russian and Slavic languages), Thai, Arabic, and Devanagari (for many languages of India and Nepal, including Hindi and Sanskrit). Writing systems for many remote languages were only devised in the last century, all of them using the alphabetic principle of one letter for one sound.

Brief History

So the English spelling system is an example of the alphabetic principle, namely that letters in the spelling represent vowel and consonant sounds in the pronunciation. However, it is probably the worst (i.e., least regular) example of an alphabetic system among languages of the world. The reasons for this are historical, and the main episodes are covered briefly here.

The English language is considered to have started when tribes (Angles, Saxons, Jutes, Franks, and Frisians) invaded Britain and defeated the Celts around 450. Their Germanic language was written using the runic alphabet. This was superseded by the Roman alphabet, which was brought to England by Christian missionaries in the sixth century. However, the (at that time) 23 letters of the Roman alphabet were inadequate to represent the 35 or so vowel and consonant sounds of Old English, and extra letters were added. It still proved necessary to use some letters (such as *c* and *g*) to represent more than one sound and to represent some sounds by combinations of letters (such as *sc*, the equivalent of present-day *sh*).

Two waves of invasions by the Vikings in 865 and 990 brought their language (Old Norse) and spelling conventions to Old English. The next invasion was the Norman conquest of 1066, bringing French language and spelling conventions.

The printing press was invented by Johannes Gutenberg in Germany in the 15th century and brought to England by William Caxton. However, many of the first printers in England came from Europe and brought European spelling conventions. Starting in the 15th century and lasting at least a couple of centuries, the Great Vowel Shift affected the whole vowel system of London English, which had been established as the accent for printing purposes. Unfortunately, while the pronunciation changed, the spelling, already standardised by printing, did not. As a result, English spelling is often a better representation of how the language was pronounced in Chaucer's day (around 1400) than in the present day.

Consonantal changes occurred at about the same time as the Great Vowel Shift; for example, what is represented by *gh* in *fought* and *night* was originally pronounced. When the sound was dropped, but the spelling remained unchanged, this gave rise to many of the silent letters in modern spelling. Similarly, starting in the 16th century, scholars changed the spelling of some words to better represent what they believed were the historical origins of the words (e.g., the *b* in *debt*). However, many of these changes were historically incorrect (e.g., the *s* in *island*).

Colonisation has brought English speakers into contact with many languages around the world. Words have been borrowed from these languages, often without changing the original spelling to conform to English patterns.

Finally, and perhaps most importantly, English spelling has never been managed. This is in contrast to many other languages that have regularised their spelling in the last century to represent modern pronunciation more accurately: Afrikaans, Albanian, Chinese, Danish, Dutch, French, German, Greek, Irish, Japanese, Malay/Indonesian, Malayalam, Norwegian, Portuguese, Romanian, Russian, Spanish, and Turkish.

This has been a necessarily very brief description of 16 centuries of influences on English spelling. For greater detail, see Brown (2014, ch. 31), Crystal (2012, 2013), Scragg (1974), and Upward and Davidson (2011). The sound-spelling correspondences of modern (British) English are given by Carney (1994).

Silent Letters

Teachers often refer to the silent letters of English spelling, that is, letters that represent no sound. But the picture is in fact more complex than that. Carney (1994) distinguishes three types of silent letter. The first is empty letters, those that represent no sound and have no other function. As a result, they could be left out and the word would still be pronounced the same. An example is the *a* of *bread*; if you leave it out, the word is spelt *bred* and pronounced the same. In this way, the homophones *bread* and *bred* would become the same.

Auxiliary letters have no sound of their own, but they do have a function of working with other letters. Magic *e*, familiar to English language teachers, is a case in point. It represents no sound in *hate, Pete, kite, rode,* and *cute.* However, it does have a function and cannot be left out. The function is to make the vowel "say its name" (e.g., the vowel in *hate* is /eɪ/, which is the name of the letter *a*). Also, it differentiates these words from *hat, pet, kit, rod,* and *cut.* The letter *h* is often auxiliary, as in *chase, phony, shave,* and *thank,* distinguishing them from *case, pony, save* and *tank.*

Finally, inert letters have no sound in the word under consideration, but they do represent a sound in morphologically related words. Thus, the *g* in *sign, resign,* and *design* represents no sound, but it does in *signature, resignation,* and *designate.*

Consequences

There are several consequences to the fact that English spelling is less regular than that of other languages. First, English language learners are likely to have native languages with more regular spelling than English. As a result, they may react with frustration to the irregularities they find in English. Similarly, teachers have to spend time correcting spelling.

Second, learners are often taught from books (i.e., in writing) and thus may pay more attention to the spelling than to the teacher's pronunciation. This often leads to spelling pronunciations, that is, pronunciations that follow on from the (misleading) spelling (e.g., pronouncing a /b/ in *debt* or an /l/ in *salmon*).

Third, it is often impossible in English to guess the pronunciation of unknown words encountered in spelling. However, as Upward (1996, p. 19) recounts, this is not the case with other, more regular languages.

A Hungarian linguist once told me of a Hungarian physics professor whose grandchild would read scientific papers aloud to him, naturally without understanding, but equally naturally conveying the sense to the listening grandfather. We must ask why we should not expect as much of English-speaking children.

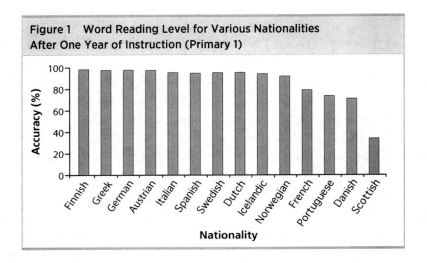

Figure 1   Word Reading Level for Various Nationalities After One Year of Instruction (Primary 1)

Finally, and perhaps most importantly, for native-English-speaking children, the amount of time spent on spelling in school is out of proportion to that spent in other countries with other native languages. Seymour, Aro, and Erskine (2003) investigated the reading levels of various nationalities (Scottish schoolchildren for English spelling) after one year of primary school. The results (Figure 1) show that English is far behind other languages.

Similarly, English language learners may be expected to spend a long time trying to master English spelling.

Is English Really Just Alphabetic?

Because of the poor sound-spelling correspondences of English, some writers, especially those interested in teaching native- and nonnative-speaking learners to read (e.g., Stirling, 2011), have proposed that there are various strategies—other than the alphabetic—for decoding written English.

The etymological system relates to the historical origins of words, especially those that came from other languages. For example, the *ch* letter combination represents the /tʃ/ sound in native (Anglo-Saxon) words, such as *church*. In words of French origin, however, it represents /ʃ/, as in *chalet*. In words of Greek origin, it is /k/ as in *chemist*. While this may be true, and interesting in a dilettante sense, it is of limited use to English language learners, who may understandably have no idea of the historical origins of words.

The graphemic system relates to typical letter patterns that are not related to sounds. For instance, there is a regular distinction in English spelling between function words (prepositions, conjunctions, auxiliary verbs, etc.) that can be written with two letters and content words (nouns, main verbs, adjectives and adverbs) that must be "bulked up" to at least three, even if they are pronounced identically or nearly identically (e.g., *be, to, by, so, in* versus *bee, too/two, buy/bye, sew/sow, inn*).

The morphological system relates to the fact that English words often contain prefixes such as *dis–, multi–,* and *hydro–,* and suffixes like *–ism, –ify,* and *–ful.* The spelling of these affixes does not normally change. This is useful in confusable pairs such as *anti–* versus *ante–, hyper–* versus *hypo–*.

Finally, the lexical system accounts for why units of meaning (morphemes) are usually spelt the same in English, regardless of differences in pronunciation. Thus, there is a *b* at the end of the word *bomb* because the *b* shows the connection between *bomb* (where it is not pronounced) and *bombard* (where it is).

Spelling Representing Pronunciation Phenomena Other Than Phonemes

The alphabetic principle means that spelling represents individual vowel and consonant sounds. Occasionally, other pronunciation phenomena are represented too.

In more informal styles of writing, spellings may represent weak forms. For instance, the spellings *fish 'n' chips* and *rock 'n' roll* indicate that the word *and* is not pronounced with its full strong form (like *band* without the *b*), but as a weak form with (1) the schwa vowel, (2) the /d/ sound elided, and (3) as a further weakening, the initial vowel elided.

One problem with the vowel schwa is that arguments are sometimes circular: This syllable is unstressed because it contains schwa, and it contains schwa because it is unstressed. In an attempt to predict the incidence of word stress, Dickerson, in many writings (1978, 1987, 1989, 1992, 2013), uses spelling rules, although they are too complex to go into in this brief chapter.

The Names of Letters

Different alphabets refer to their letters in different ways. In the Thai alphabet, letters are referred to by the sound they make in initial position, followed by the /ɔ:/ vowel. Thus, for instance, *s* is called /sɔ:/. (This is, in fact, a simplification, as there are more than one *s* letters, with different tonal implications in this tonal language.) Similarly, in Arabic, letters are referred to by their sound followed by different groupings of sounds. For instance, *s* is referred to as *seen*.

This is possible in the Thai and Arabic alphabets because the correspondence between letters and sounds is regular. In English, on the other hand, the correspondence is less regular, and the names of letters are similarly less regular. The letter *s*, for example, is known by the name /ɛs/, that is, by the typical sound represented by the letter, preceded by the vowel /e/. The same is true of *f, l, m, n,* and *x.* However, *g* is known as /dʒi/, that is, the sound /dʒ/ (which is not the most common sound represented by *g*) followed by the vowel /i/. A similar pattern occurs for *b, c, d, p, t,* and *v* (and *z* for Americans).

This lack of a rationale for the naming of letters leads to confusion for some learners between the name of the letter and the sound the letter typically represents. Thus native-speaking children may misspell *sky* as *ski*, not because they confuse the /aɪ/ and /i/ vowels, but because *sk* represents /sk/ and /aɪ/ is the name of the letter *i*. This is similar to the use of numerals and other devices in SMS text language, as in the title of Crystal's (2009) book *Txtng: The Gr8 Db8*.

Punctuation

Punctuation is used in writing to give an indication of several possible pronunciation features (see the Punctuation subsection under Exercises later in the chapter). However, English punctuation has never been standardised. While some conventions are fixed (e.g., a full-stop, question mark, or exclamation mark at the end of a sentence), other practices are not, and they change over time. At present, dashes and bullets seem to be in, while semicolons and apostrophes seem to be out. As Carey (1958) observed, punctuation is governed "two-thirds by rule and one-third by personal taste" (p. 15).

Exercises

The following exercises are aimed at helping learners distinguish sounds from spellings in English, explore the sound-spelling correspondences, and practise the pronunciation of English sounds and words. The final exercise relates to the interface between punctuation and pronunciation. Answers have not been given where they would be obvious to readers of this book (but not to learners). These exercises can easily be adapted to suit learners at various levels. Readers can also create their own versions along the same lines as those given.

Homophones

Homophones are words that are pronounced the same but spelt differently (see Chapter 1). They exist in English because of the poor sound-spelling correspondence; homophones are impossible in languages with regular correspondences. In the following passage, some words have been wrongly spelt as their homophone. Identify and correct them.

> Ethical dealings, or fare trade, means doing what is write when you bye and cell products or services. Unfortunately, there are many businesspeople who brake promises, fail to meat commitments, and holed out for two high a price. For every

sail that they make, they will try all weighs and means to make a healthy prophet, down the last scent. They may, in effect, steel from the poor and pray on helpless old people. But they may eventually be the reel losers, as the authorities may sees their assets and, because their activities are just plane criminal, they may be throne in jail and maid to pay reparation.

By having students identify and correct spellings, you can cover several spelling and pronunciation phenomena:

- Because learners are often more influenced by spelling than by sound, some may refuse to acknowledge that, for instance, *profit* and *prophet* have the same pronunciation.

- Similarly, some learners may refuse to believe that there is no /w/ sound in *write* or even that the *gh* represents no sound in *weighs* (although this is clear because they are homophonous with *right* and *ways*).

- You can ask learners if it seems sensible that there is no *e* in *hold*, but one in *holed* (because it is a past tense), or that there is no *w* in *too*, but one in *two* (because it is related to *twice, twelve, twenty, twins*, etc.).

- Alternative sound-to-spelling patterns may be examined, for example, the *aCe* and *aiC* patterns in *fare/fair, sale/sail, plane/plain*, and *made/maid*.

- At a deeper level, you could ask which of alternative spellings seems more logical or regular (e.g., *sent, cent, scent*).

Silent Letters
Silent letters are those that represent no sound in the word. Identify the silent letters in the following words. Add together the silent letters in each row to give you a word and a 14-word quotation. Thus the first word is *a*. (Unfortunately, *key* is the only word for silent *y*!)

1. *bread*
2. *island, key, hymn, young, autumn, key, mnemonic*
3. *friend, debris*
4. *breath*
5. *write, nourish, iron, handsome*
6. *key, leopard, build*
7. *guard, aisle, have*
8. *who, chasm, bye, damn*

9. *key, cousin, guild*

10. *scent, thread, column, soften*

11. *chassis, receipt, unique, salmon, would*

12. *ballet, school, give*

13. *jeopardy, mortgage, honest, dye, metier*

14. *foetus, solemn, plaque*

Answer

"A synonym is a word you use when you can't spell the other one" (Baltasar Gracián, 17th-century Spanish writer). With *foetus*, notice that American spelling (*fetus*) often eliminates these silent letters.

Permissible Spellings and Permissible Pronunciations

Many of the exercises in this section relate to the distinction between sounds and spellings, a distinction that must be understood for English because of the poor correspondence between the two. This exercise examines spelling patterns that are impossible for various reasons and pronunciation patterns that are impossible for various reasons (which may therefore also be represented here by impossible spellings). It is based on a similar exercise in Kenworthy (1987).

Below are given, in spelling, some words that do not exist in English. Some are possible (potential) words, both in spelling and in pronunciation. The rest are impossible, either because they contain impossible spelling patterns or because they contain impossible pronunciation patterns (which may therefore also be represented here by impossible spellings). They will therefore seem "un-English".

Classify each example into one of the above three categories (impossible for spelling reasons, impossible for pronunciation reasons, possible/potential), with an explanation.

bwang	panj	spwuck
ckam	plarh	swick
crefted	quemple	tchemp
damk	sboin	tlank
ferrowh	scatch	trong
hent	shrisk	troqu
juspy	shwander	twest
ngist	spramp	whilm

Answer

The following words are impossible:

For Spelling Reasons

ckam: The spelling sequence *ck* (representing /k/) occurs only at the ends of words (in fact, syllables), as in *swick*.

ferrowh: The spelling sequence *wh* (representing either /w/ as in *whim* or /h/ as in *whole*) occurs only at the beginnings of words, as in *whilm*.

panj: The letter *j* (representing /dʒ/) occurs only at the beginnings of words, as in *juspy*.

tchemp: the spelling sequence *tch* (representing /tʃ/) occurs only at the ends of words after short vowels, as in *scatch*. The only exceptions to this are *much, rich, such*, and *which*. Also *attach*, and this accounts for the common wrong (but more regular) spelling *attatch*.

troqu: The spelling sequence *qu* (representing either /kw/ as in *quick*, or /k/ as in *quiche*) occurs only at the beginnings of words, as in *quemple*. Finally, it would require an *e*, as in *unique*. Also, /kw/ is impossible as a final cluster.

For Pronunciation Reasons

bwang: /bw/ is impossible as an initial cluster in English, thus the spelling *bw–* is similarly impossible.

damk: /mk/ is impossible as a final cluster in English, thus the spelling *–mk* is similarly impossible.

ngist: /ŋ/ is impossible as an initial consonant in English, thus the spelling *ng–* is similarly impossible.

plarh: /h/ is impossible in syllable-final position in English. While the letter *h* may occur at the ends of English words, it is always part of a two-letter combination (*English, graph, laugh, myth, rich*) or silent (*cheetah*).

sboin: /sb/ is impossible as an initial cluster in English, thus the spelling *sb–* is similarly impossible.

shwander: /ʃw/ is impossible as an initial cluster in English, thus the spelling *shw–* is similarly impossible.

spwuck: /spw/ is impossible as an initial cluster in English, thus the spelling *spw–* is similarly impossible.

tlank: /tl/ is impossible as an initial cluster in English, thus the spelling *tl–* is similarly impossible.

All the other examples are potential words or syllables.

Identifying Sounds

Our yachtsman is going island-hopping in the South Pacific, following the sea lanes and stopping only at those islands with the /ɛ/ sound, as in *best*, on the way to his home marina in New Zealand. Which islands does he go via?

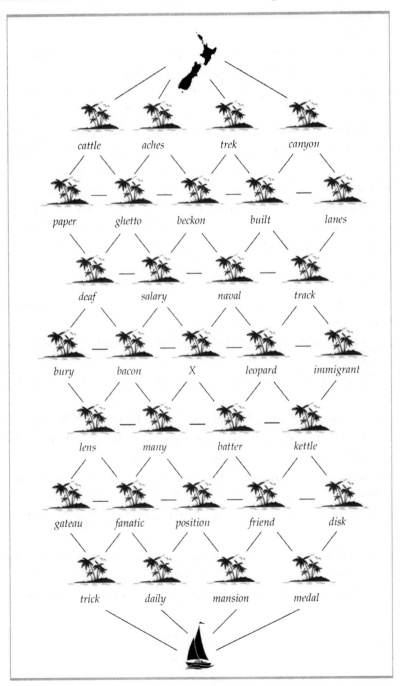

Answer

The answer is *medal, friend, kettle, leopard, X, many, lens, bury, deaf, ghetto, beckon, trek.* In discussing the answer, you can do the following:

- Compare some /ɛ/ words with minimal pair words with /ɪ/: *belt/built, trek/ trick, emigrant/immigrant, possession/position, desk/disk.*

- Compare some /ɛ/ words with minimal pair words with /eɪ/: *Delhi/daily, lens/ lanes, beckon/bacon, pepper/paper, Neville/naval, X/aches.*

- Compare some /ɛ/ words with minimal pair words with /æ/: *mention/mansion, trek/track, ghetto/gateau, phonetic/fanatic, better/batter, celery/salary, kettle/cattle, Kenyan/canyon.*

- List some /ɛ/ words with irregular spellings: *leopard, many, bury, deaf.*

- Derive the main spelling patterns for these sounds:
  - /ɛ/: *e, ea,* some individual peculiarities
  - /æ/: *a*
  - /ɪ/: *i*
  - /eɪ/: *aCV, ai*

The main sound-spelling correspondences for (British) English are given by Carney (1994). Minimal pairs for (British) English are given by Higgins (2014). Similar game formats, that can easily be adapted to highlight features of pronunciation and/or spelling, can be found in Brown (2005) and Hancock (1995).

The Various Pronunciations of Past Tense *–(e)d and* Plural *–(e)s Endings*

While the spelling of the past tense *–(e)d* and plural *–(e)s* endings does not change, they may represent different pronunciations (see Chapter 7). However, many learners have problems with the /ɪd/ and /ɪz/ pronunciations, as in *wanted* and *wishes.* Since the /ɪd/ and /ɪz/ endings involve a vowel, and thus an extra syllable, one way to practise this is to focus on the number of syllables rather than the sounds, a technique favoured by Gilbert (2012), who also encourages kinaesthetics by requiring learners to tap the syllables on the desk.

All of the following words end in *–(e)d* or *–(e)s.* Sort them according to the number of syllables they contain.

added	demands	identified	recommended
annoyed	divided	inches	recommends
applied	elephants	landed	reported
approaches	emergencies	laughed	reports
ashes	experiments	multiplied	subtracted
buys	finished	organised	talked
calculators	finishes	overreaches	teachers
celebrated	freed	played	teaches
confessed	garages	quizzes	tested
connects	groups	raced	toes
dedicated	guarantees	races	tried
delivered	hates	ranged	villages
demanded	hats	rates	wished

WORDS WITH ONE SYLLABLE	WORDS WITH TWO SYLLABLES	WORDS WITH THREE SYLLABLES	WORDS WITH FOUR SYLLABLES
O	OO	OOO	OOOO

This exercise naturally leads to a discussion of word stress because, even if the words have the same number of syllables, they may not have the same stress pattern. For instance, in the three-syllable words, *elephants* has stress on the first syllable (Ooo), *approaches* on the second (oOo), and *guarantees* on the third (ooO).

The Various Pronunciations of ch

All the following words contain the letters *ch*. However, this sequence may represent /tʃ/ (usually in native English, Anglo-Saxon, words), /ʃ/ (usually in words borrowed from French), or /k/ (usually in words borrowed from Greek). Sort them into the right letterboxes.

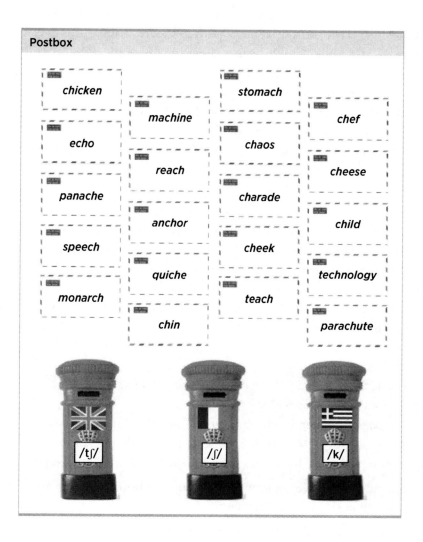

Punctuation

In the following short passage from *Alice's Adventures in Wonderland* (Carroll, 1865), Alice is walking along a road when she comes to a fork. The Cheshire Cat is sitting in a tree. Most of the punctuation has been omitted. Can you insert the punctuation?

> The Cat only grinned when it saw Alice it looked good-natured she thought still it had very long claws and a great many teeth so she felt that it ought to be treated with respect Cheshire Puss she began rather timidly as she did not at all know whether it would like the name however it only grinned a little wider come it's pleased so far thought Alice and she went on would you tell me please which way I ought to go from here that depends a good deal on where you want to get to said the Cat I don't much care where said Alice then it doesn't matter which way you go said the Cat so long as I get somewhere Alice added as an explanation oh you're sure to do that said the Cat if you only walk long enough

Answer

The original passage as punctuated in *Alice's Adventures in Wonderland*:

The Cat only grinned when it saw Alice. It looked good-natured, she thought: still it had VERY long claws and a great many teeth, so she felt that it ought to be treated with respect.

"Cheshire Puss," she began, rather timidly, as she did not at all know whether it would like the name: however, it only grinned a little wider. "Come, it's pleased so far," thought Alice, and she went on. "Would you tell me, please, which way I ought to go from here?"

"That depends a good deal on where you want to get to," said the Cat.

"I don't much care where—" said Alice.

"Then it doesn't matter which way you go," said the Cat.

"—so long as I get SOMEWHERE," Alice added as an explanation.

"Oh, you're sure to do that," said the Cat, "if you only walk long enough."

The punctuation conveys pronunciation information, including the following (some of which are covered in Chapter 5):

- Commas, full-stops, and paragraph breaks indicate short, medium, and long pauses, respectively, usually demarcating tone groups. They usually occur at grammatical boundaries and thus show what belongs together. It is possible to misread the first line *The Cat only grinned. When it saw Alice, it looked good-natured. She thought still it had VERY long claws.*

- Commas may also separate parenthetical stretches, which are said on lowered intonation range (key), as in *rather timidly.*

- Quotation marks indicate what is said, and especially where there is a change of speaker and a new paragraph, this normally starts with heightened key (e.g., *"Cheshire Puss," she began*).

- Paragraph breaks, manifested by long pauses and heightened key, may indicate a change of speaker, as between the following two lines: *"Would you tell me, please, which way I ought to go from here?"* and *"That depends a good deal on where you want to get to."* Without the heightened key, it would sound as though Alice was continuing to speak.

- Question marks indicate questions, and the question here (*"Would you tell me, please, which way I ought to go from here?"*) is said with rising final tone.

- Dashes (or ellipsis) indicate unfinished speech, said on a non-falling (probably level) tone (*"I don't much care where—" said Alice*).

- The words *very* and *somewhere* are written in all capitals here (alternatively, bold, italics, or underline) to show they are emphasised, and they receive the large intonation movement (tonic).

Conclusion

English spelling is a problem for learners precisely because it is the spelling of English, where the sound-spelling correspondence is poor. This is a consequence of 16 centuries of unmanaged spelling. Spelling may be far less of a problem in learners' native languages. Learners often find it difficult to separate English spelling from sounds, and spelling pronunciations result. The exercises presented here are aimed at exploring both these spelling problems.

Punctuation is much more idiosyncratic in nature, but has some implications for pronunciation.

References

Brown, A. (2005). *Sounds, symbols and spellings*. Singapore: McGraw-Hill.

Brown, A. (2014). *Pronunciation and phonetics: A practical guide for English language teachers*. New York, NY: Routledge.

Carey, G. V. (1958). *Mind the stop: A brief guide to punctuation*. Cambridge, England: Cambridge University Press.

Carney, E. (1994). *A survey of English spelling*. London, England: Routledge.

Carroll, L. (1865). *Alice's adventures in wonderland*. London, England: Macmillan.

Crystal, D. (2009). *Txtng: The Gr8 Db8*. Oxford, England: Oxford University Press.

Crystal, D. (2012). *Spell it out: The singular story of English spelling*. London, England: Profile Books.

Crystal, D. (2013). *The story of English in 100 words*. London, England: Profile Books.

Dickerson, W. B. (1978). English orthography: A guide to word stress and vowel quality. *International Review of Applied Linguistics in Language Teaching, 16,* 127–147.

Dickerson, W. B. (1987). Orthography as a pronunciation resource. *World Englishes, 6,* 11–20.

Dickerson, W. B. (1989). *Stress in the speech stream: The rhythm of spoken English.* Urbana, IL: University of Illinois Press.

Dickerson, W. B. (1992). Orthography: A window on the world of sound. In A. Brown (Ed.), *Approaches to pronunciation teaching* (pp. 103–117). London, England: British Council and Macmillan.

Dickerson, W. B. (2013). Prediction in pronunciation teaching. In C. A. Chapelle (Ed.), *The encyclopedia of applied linguistics* (pp. 4638–4645). Hoboken, NJ: Wiley-Blackwell.

Gilbert, J. B. (2012). *Clear speech: Pronunciation and listening comprehension in North American English* (4th ed.). New York, NY: Cambridge University Press.

Hancock, M. (1995). *Pronunciation games.* Cambridge, England: Cambridge University Press.

Higgins, J. (2014). *Minimal pairs for English RP.* Retrieved from http://myweb.tiscali .co.uk/wordscape/wordlist/minimal.html

Kenworthy, J. (1987). *Teaching English pronunciation.* Harlow, England: Longman.

Scragg, D. G. (1974). *A history of English spelling.* Manchester, England: Manchester University Press.

Seymour, P. H. K., Aro, M., & Erskine, J. (2003). Foundation literacy acquisition in European orthographies. *British Journal of Psychology, 94,* 143–174.

Stirling, J. (2011). *Teaching spelling to English language learners.* Raleigh, NC: Lulu.

Upward, C. (1996). *English spelling: The need for a psycho-historical perspective.* Birmingham, England: Aston University, Institute for the Study of Language & Society. Retrieved from http://spellingsociety.org/uploaded_books/b4aston4.pdf

Upward, C., & Davidson, G. (2011). *The history of English spelling.* Chichester, England: Wiley-Blackwell.

CONCLUSION

The Integration of Pronunciation and Real Teaching Contexts

I started the Introduction to this book with the question: Where are we now? I believe that many of you may have felt the same trepidation about incorporating pronunciation into your lessons as I did. As I mentioned in the introduction, I had a vague but powerful fear that, in fact, I was patently unqualified to help students achieve intelligibility because I did not know the International Phonetic Alphabet (IPA.) When I was asked to teach an intermediate pronunciation course at my new college, I was nervous. However, as an adjunct, I was also desperate for hours. So, I swallowed my fear of the IPA and told the director that I would be happy to teach the class.

Throughout that semester, as my students and I worked through the course book, I was astounded to learn that the IPA was only part of the picture and that teaching pronunciation actually meant rendering transparent all the things I naturally did as a proficient English speaker to make my message clear to my listeners. My understanding of English pronunciation was inflated beyond a shaky grasp of the sound system of English consonant and vowel phonemes to a more global vision of English pronunciation as a set of interrelated core features. Gilbert (2008) refers to these features as

> rhythmic and melodic signals [which] serve as "road signs" to help the listener follow the intentions of the speaker. These signals communicate emphasis and make clear the relationship between ideas so that listeners can readily identify these relationships and understand the speaker's meaning. (Gilbert, 2008, p. 2)

However, while this realization was a professional awakening of sorts for me, it wasn't until a few years later that I recognized that not only could I teach pronunciation, but it was so important that I should not confine my teaching to designated pronunciation classes. I found myself sneaking pronunciation instruction into my TOEFL prep and comprehensive English lessons as I came to understand that all of my students benefited from pronunciation instruction, no matter what class they had registered for.

I hope the chapters in this book have helped alleviate some of the anxiety the thought of squeezing pronunciation into your already over-packed curricula might raise. The authors' theory-based suggestions for activities are easily adaptable to a wide-variety of contexts and need not consume a huge amount of class time. Rather, the goal is to make pronunciation such an integral part of your vocabulary, speaking, listening, grammar, reading or spelling lessons that in a short time you won't be able to imagine teaching without it.

Since we started this book with a question, perhaps we can finish with one: Where do we go from here? Clearly, the most logical response is, quite simply, for teachers to put the suggestions raised in this book into action in the classroom. Experiment with different activities and adapt them until they meet the needs of your students. Then share them with other teachers. Also, don't be afraid to demand more from materials writers and publishers. Urge curriculum designers to provide the scaffolding for assimilating pronunciation in more systematic and explicit ways, and insist on textbooks that come with pronunciation already seamlessly integrated into lessons (Gilbert, 2010). The authors of this book have demonstrated that including pronunciation instruction into other skills instruction benefits not only students' oral skills, but also their vocabulary acquisition, listening skills, grammatical accuracy, reading skills, and spelling. Therefore, the last question I want to ask is: What are we waiting for?

References

Gilbert, J. (2008). *Teaching pronunciation: Using the prosody pyramid.* Cambridge, England: Cambridge University Press.

Gilbert, J. (2010). Pronunciation as orphan: What can be done? *As We Speak, 43,* 3–7.S